NIK NAZMI NIK AHMAD

MOVING FORWARD

MALAYS FOR THE 21ST CENTURY

© 2019 Marshall Cavendish International (Asia) Private Limited
Text © Nik Nazmi Nik Ahmad

First published in 2010 by Marshall Cavendish Editions
This new edition published in 2019 by Marshall Cavendish Editions
An imprint of Marshall Cavendish International

All rights reserved

No part of this publication may be reproduced, stored in a retrieval system or transmitted, in any form or by any means, electronic, mechanical, photocopying, recording or otherwise, without the prior permission of the copyright owner. Requests for permission should be addressed to the Publisher, Marshall Cavendish International (Asia) Private Limited, 1 New Industrial Road, Singapore 536196.
Tel: (65) 6213 9300 E-mail: genref@sg.marshallcavendish.com
Website: www.marshallcavendish.com/genref

The publisher makes no representation or warranties with respect to the contents of this book, and specifically disclaims any implied warranties or merchantability or fitness for any particular purpose, and shall in no event be liable for any loss of profit or any other commercial damage, including but not limited to special, incidental, consequential, or other damages.

Other Marshall Cavendish Offices:
Marshall Cavendish Corporation, 99 White Plains Road, Tarrytown NY 10591-9001, USA • Marshall Cavendish International (Thailand) Co Ltd, 253 Asoke, 12th Flr, Sukhumvit 21 Road, Klongtoey Nua, Wattana, Bangkok 10110, Thailand • Marshall Cavendish (Malaysia) Sdn Bhd, Times Subang, Lot 46, Subang Hi-Tech Industrial Park, Batu Tiga, 40000 Shah Alam, Selangor Darul Ehsan, Malaysia.

Marshall Cavendish is a registered trademark of Times Publishing Limited

National Library Board, Singapore Cataloguing-in-Publication Data

Name(s): Nazmi Nik Ahmad, Nik.
Title: Moving forward : Malays for the 21st century / Nik Nazmi Nik Ahmad.
Description: Singapore : Marshall Cavendish Editions, 2019.
Identifier(s): OCN 1089818290 | ISBN 978-981-48-4187-0 (paperback)
Subject(s): LCSH: Malays (Asian people)--21st century. | Malays (Asian people)--Social life and customs. | Malays (Asian people)--Politics and government. | Malays (Asian people)--Malaysia--Social life and customs.
Classification: DDC 305.89928--dc23

Printed in Singapore

To my parents

CONTENTS

LIST OF ABBREVIATIONS   7
PREFACE TO THIS EDITION   9
ACKNOWLEDGEMENTS   13

INTRODUCTION   17

A NEW POLITICAL PARADIGM   23
    8 March 2008: Which Way Forward?   24
    The New Politics   28
    Why Keadilan?   34

TOWARDS A PEOPLE'S ECONOMY   40
    The NEP: A Reconsideration   41
    The GLCs, Malays and Business   59
    A People's Economy: The Selangor Experience   65

THE EDUCATION QUESTION   71
    A Dynamic and Equitable Education Policy   72
    Other Men's Tongues: The Vernacular Issue   82
    The Mentari Project   87

ISLAM IN A MULTICULTURAL SOCIETY   92
    Celebrating Our Tradition of Moderation   93
    No Compulsion: Non-Muslims and Islam in Malaysia   107

THE SOCIAL REVOLUTION   110
    Marriage and Family Life   111
    Suffer the Young   115
    A Glimpse into Seri Setia   120

CONCLUSION   124
    The Dream That is Malaysia   125

POSTSCRIPT   134
    To Move Malaysia Forward   135

SELECT BIBLIOGRAPHY   147
ABOUT THE AUTHOR   150

LIST OF ABBREVIATIONS

AMCJA	All Malaya Council for Joint Action
AP	Approved Permit
BCIC	Bumiputera Commercial and Industrial Community
BTN	Biro Tata Negara (National Civics Bureau)
DAP	Democratic Action Party
EPU	Economic Planning Unit of the Prime Minister's Department
Gerakan	Parti Gerakan Rakyat Malaysia (Malaysian People's Movement Party)
GLC	Government-Linked Company
HICOM	Heavy Industries Corporation of Malaysia Berhad
IMP	Independence of Malaya Party
Keadilan	Parti Keadilan Rakyat (People's Justice Party)
MARA	Majlis Amanah Rakyat (People's Trust Council)
MCKK	The Malay College Kuala Kangsar
MBPJ	Majlis Bandaraya Petaling Jaya (Petaling Jaya City Council)
NEP	New Economic Policy
PAS	Parti Islam SeMalaysia (Pan Malaysian Islamic Party)
PNB	Permodalan Nasional Berhad (National Equity Corporation)
PR	Pakatan Rakyat (People's Pact/People's Alliance); made up of Keadilan, DAP and PAS
PSD	Public Services Department
PUTERA	Pusat Tenaga Rakyat (People's Action Centre)
SPM	Sijil Pelajaran Malaysia (Malaysian Certificate of Education)
STPM	Sijil Tinggi Pelajaran Malaysia (Malaysian Higher Certificate of Education)
UMNO	United Malays National Organisation
UPSR	Ujian Penilaian Sekolah Rendah (Primary School Assessment Test)

PREFACE TO THIS EDITION

Many people were surprised when *Moving Forward: Malays for the 21st Century* was published a decade ago. At the time, I was (and still am) pushing for a more progressive paradigm where Malaysians would be at ease with their country's diversity. This led some to question me: Why then did I write a book addressing the Malays specifically? Wasn't this a contradiction in terms?

As *Moving Forward* argues, the state of mind of the Malays is crucial if any change in Malaysia is to be sustainable. Malays are by sheer number the biggest community in the country; we are also the fastest growing. Constitutionally, historically and culturally, we occupy a special position in Malaysia.

I believe that the community's own future is best assured with progressive politics, and that the fate of such progressive politics in Malaysia is in the hands of the Malays.

I wrote these things because UMNO was increasingly playing the race and religion card following the loss of Barisan Nasional's two-thirds majority in 2008. I was the youngest legislator to be elected that year. I was also appointed Political Secretary to the first non-UMNO Menteri Besar of Selangor and experienced first-hand the challenges in convincing the Malays that a different kind of future was possible.

Ten years later at the 2018 General Election, Barisan Nasional lost power for the first time in Malaysia's history. This time, I won as an

MP and led the new Pakatan Harapan coalition's Youth Wing as well as the KEADILAN Youth. I journeyed to Malay villages in Terengganu and deep in the heart of Perak, to low-cost flats in the Klang Valley and Johor Bahru, to Dayak longhouses in Sarawak and Bumiputera communities in the interior of Sabah.

Pakatan Harapan and our ally in Sabah, WARISAN, won a majority of the Parliamentary seats. But unlike in 2013, when the PAS (Pan-Malaysian Islamic Party) was in Pakatan Rakyat and we obtained a majority in the popular vote, this time the three-way contests across the country led to a lower share for Pakatan Harapan.

PAS was almost entirely wiped out on the west coast, but on the east coast, it retained Kelantan and took back Terengganu after 14 years. Pakatan Harapan was impressive on the west coast—but only from Selangor southwards. UMNO and pockets of PAS remained strong in Perak, Kedah, Perlis and even mainland Penang.

WARISAN and Pakatan Harapan did well among the Muslim Bumiputeras in the east coast of Sabah, but predictably, Pakatan Harapan failed to make inroads among the Muslim Bumiputeras in Sarawak. This seems ironic, since Sarawakians, like Sabahans, have always been comfortable with social diversity—a trait commonly associated with Pakatan Harapan. At the same time, many Dayak constituencies voted for Pakatan Harapan and independent candidates.

Older, hopefully wiser and definitely more overweight, I have reflected on these experiences as the Pakatan Harapan federal government announced its first cabinet, introduced its first budget and sought to implement policies that stayed true to its manifesto.

On WhatsApp groups and my Facebook page as well as mamak shops, the Malay community across all segments became more worried. The issues of LGBT rights and child marriage exposed the deep divide in Malaysian society. This came to a head when the government spoke of ratifying the International Convention on the Elimination of All Forms of Racial Discrimination (ICERD)—a convention ratified by all

Muslim majority countries except for Malaysia and Brunei—resulting in a massive rally combining PAS, UMNO and right-wing NGOs.

In light of these events, *Moving Forward* is just as relevant today as it was in 2009. While the content remains largely the same as it was when first published, this edition includes an updated conclusion to reflect on the book's ideas in light of the progress we have achieved and the new challenges we face today.

Kuala Lumpur
2019

ACKNOWLEDGEMENTS

This book is a culmination of a long process that involved both intellectual reflection and a practical participation in politics. I strongly believe there is value in balancing the two. As one of the greatest Muslim scholars, Abu Hamid al-Ghazali once said, "Knowledge without action is madness while action without knowledge is pointless." It is my sincere hope that my writing demonstrates my knowledge put into action and vice-versa.

Writing *Moving Forward* became a source of therapy as I became more exposed to the rough-and-tumble world of politics. It provided me with the time and space to reflect, indeed to remind myself of the ideals that got me involved in public service in the first place.

Many people have contributed in various ways to make this book a reality and it would be remiss of me not to acknowledge them here.

I am forever grateful to Allahyarham Adlan Benan Omar, the most brilliant Malaysian of his generation, not only for getting me into politics but for encouraging me to write and provoking me to always think critically. Khalid Jaafar also played an important role by giving me a column in what was thwen known as *Berita Keadilan* that allowed me to formulate many thoughts, which have now culminated in this book.

Both Steven Gan of *Malaysiakini* and Ho Kay Tat who was Chief Editor of *The Sun* and *The Edge* newspapers gave me the space to develop my writing and argue many of the basic positions that underlie the general theme of this book. I must also thank Leslie Lau of *The Malaysian Insider* for inviting me to be a columnist on that website.

Parts of *Moving Forward* include portions from some previously published essays. These include 'Saying Yes to Non-Racial Affirmative Action' which was originally published in *Malaysiakini*; 'Where Are the Young Malays?' in *The Edge*; 'The Family, the State and Globalisation' in *Asia Times Online* and a jointly-written essay with Nurul Izzah Anwar, 'Working for Malaysia's Future' in *The Malaysian Insider*.

Karim Raslan deserves a special mention for persuading me to keep on writing no matter how tied down I got with politics, and for suggesting that I write something on the Malays.

I must also record my appreciation to Christine Chong of Marshall Cavendish Malaysia for so quickly and enthusiastically agreeing to publish my work.

I would like to thank my friends, Tunku 'Abidin Muhriz and Hafiz Noor Shams for listening to my thoughts when I initially had the idea for writing *Moving Forward*. Having shared so many projects that did not take off, I have to give them credit for continuing to provide me with the inputs that led to the birth of this book.

After I finished the initial draft, Tunku 'Abidin and Hafiz along with Lynn Kuok, Ng Boon Ka, Najwan Halimi, Imran Karim, Imran Idris, Saifullah Zulkifli and Hizami Iskandar took time off from their busy schedules to read through and comment on the draft. Keith Leong was especially pivotal in restructuring the book to make it more coherent while playing the role of an intellectual sparring partner. Fahda Nur Ahmad Kamar also provided me with crucial advice at the final stage of the book. I am privileged to know this excellent group of young Malaysians who exemplify the best that Malaysia has to offer.

Mawarni Hassan's experience in education has been a useful source of reference for my elaborations on the subject in *Moving Forward*. More importantly however, is the fact that Mawarni and her family have sacrificed so much to make the Mentari Project a success. This was a product of not only our extensive brainstorming, but also their constant plodding, week in and week out, even after I was elected as assemblyman for Seri Setia and could not devote as much attention to the project as I did before.

I have been blessed with the privilege of serving Malaysia under two towering personalities, Datuk Seri Anwar Ibrahim and Tan Sri Dato' Abdul Khalid Ibrahim. Datuk Seri Anwar taught me never to forget my intellectual and spiritual roots. He is also a constant reminder of the importance of not losing faith in our ideals even while bogged down in the muck and grime of politics.

Tan Sri Khalid contributed to my vision for Malaysia's future and gave me the latitude to write even as I juggled so many responsibilities as his Political Secretary. He has also taught me the invaluable lesson of seeing public life as a service of, for and by the people. In addition, long-time trade unionist, Syed Shahir Syed Mohamud, my Parti Keadilan Rakyat Division Chief has taught me never to give up on the struggle and provided the space for me to learn and develop.

My father, who spurred my interest in reading particularly on the subjects of religion, history, politics and economics from a very young age, also showed me the need to be passionate in what I believe in. Our different generational perspectives on Malay issues are a useful case study on how the Malay society has evolved from the 20th to the 21st century. Both my parents have vigorously supported me all my life, even when I chose the path less taken and to them, I owe that inextinguishable debt children bear to their parents.

The unwavering support of my wife, Imaan, not only for this project but for all my other endeavours has been a great source of strength. She too, was willing to lend an ear to my ideas and read through my drafts, making them more accessible with her suggestions. *Moving Forward* is a better book because of her. She has had to patiently put up with a husband who was not only busy with politics but with writing a book, all the while grappling with her own medical career.

There are others who have contributed to *Moving Foward* in various ways who I am regrettably unable to name. Without their help, this book would never have been written. Their names, where mentioned in this book have been changed to protect them.

Needless to say, any errors or mistakes are entirely my own.

INTRODUCTION

This book is about a young man's hopes and dreams for the Malay community. It is about his hope that they can rise from the stagnation that they have found themselves in today. It tells of his dream that they can, one day, embrace and be embraced by a larger Malaysian national ethos even as their Malay identity grows from strength to strength.

I am aware that this topic has been done to death, but that in no way excuses me from my duty to speak up for my people and my country. The same goes for all Malaysians when the situation calls for it—something that is becoming increasingly the case of late. Until and unless Malays and all Malaysians are willing to truly speak their mind, then our country will remain condemned to mediocrity. It is to the former that this book is addressed, but I hope that what I have written here is also something the latter can take cognisance of and dare I say, draw inspiration from.

It is increasingly obvious that the Malaysian Malays of the 21st century are at a crossroads. The Malay archipelago has traditionally always been part of the international trading network and hence, the fortunes of the community are inevitably tied to changes at the global stage. As the scenario for the world, including Malaysia, evolves rapidly, Malaysians must grapple with a very different set of challenges as well.

In many ways, when the country achieved Merdeka (Independence), Malaysia was an improbable nation marked by innumerable paradoxes.

A fractured society divided by race, religion and economic class, yet blessed with abundant resources and rich cultures, it undertook a unique constitutional consensus that was agreed upon by the different communities to enable the country to gain independence.

Within a decade, however, the unresolved problems related to our colonial experience reared their ugly heads and the consensus came under threat. In response, a new compromise—embodied by the NEP—was forged with the spirit of consensus that led us to freedom.

Yet, this compromise has now become a sacred cow of sorts, one that must not be questioned by anyone. Even as the society has evolved and new challenges have emerged, the government has decided to maintain the status quo at all costs—even when fresh solutions are needed—all in the name of Malay interests.

Worse still, race continues to be used as a divisive tool in politics to perpetuate a sense of fear and foreboding among ordinary Malaysians while the world moves on. Culture wars that are half a century old continue to be waged, while the battles that we need to fight to ensure that the Malays and Malaysia move forward continue to be ignored.

But the 12th Malaysian General Elections on 8 March, 2008 brought about a new opening. It brought to the fore a new generation of Malays that can hope for a different Malaysia and break the politics of fear.

The results of the 12th General Elections can be interpreted in many ways, but certainly it proved that the Malays could support moving away from the race-based system if communicated in the right way (although admittedly, other factors such as the weak BN leadership, a united Opposition, the rise of new media and spiralling prices, had also contributed to this positive outcome).

I have written many articles on various Malay issues and have thought long and hard about articulating an overall outlook on how Malays can move forward. A few friends who became aware of this then asked me to put these thoughts down in a book.

I hesitated at first, since I did not know how useful my contribution would be to this controversial and complex subject. In addition, I cannot deny that I have also been a beneficiary of the NEP: I was educated at an elite all-Malay institution, the MCKK and received a GLC scholarship reserved for Bumiputeras. But my friends persuaded me to complete this book since they felt that it would offer a useful perspective on the issue.

Yes, I have benefited from the NEP and acknowledge as much throughout the book. I accept the policy's positive contributions. However, I believe that it is to the credit of the NEP that the Malays who have been empowered by the policy now realise that we need to come up with alternatives if the Malays are to face the challenges of the 21st century. The most compelling reason to do away with the NEP now is that it has worked for a great many Malays, but another model is now needed to help the Malays that have not benefited as well as their non-Malay compatriots in need.

I believe it is crucial to examine the questions raised in this book, and for these questions to be evaluated on their merits. I have tried to straddle my writing between a purely academic exercise and a polemical treatise, preferring to keep references to a minimum while at the same time trying to support my arguments with facts.

In my conversations with Malays from all walks of life, be they my friends who are working in GLCs, young graduates trying their hand at small businesses, hawkers finding some space to make a living or single mothers looking for jobs to support their children, I have found that much of their concerns are not particularly 'Malay'. Their sentiments are no different from other Malaysians in similar situations and indeed, are *Malaysian* concerns.

I accept that race is still relevant even in the 21st century. People will always be conscious of their roots and heritage. Nevertheless, it is possible to move away from our obsession with race. It is possible for our policies to be developed based on merit and need, which will foster

Malay progress at the same time. Ethnicity ought to remain a helpful and powerful marker of identity, but policies should be formulated with common challenges as the dominant consideration. It should never be a reason to exclude people or make them feel unwanted in the country of their birth.

How would such a change benefit the Malays? By shifting to a needs-based affirmative action programme, the plight of Malays who truly deserve assistance will continue to be addressed, while the culture of dependency that has emerged from the NEP will be dismantled. By moving to an inclusive political system based on cooperation rather than confrontation, the Malays can get broader support from all the communities to face the multiple challenges that globalisation brings.

The NEP is and always was a top-down phenomenon. Even when Mahathir shifted the NEP to be driven by the private instead of the public sector, it was still essentially a government-led, trickle-down form of ersatz capitalism. With the changing world today, we need to make Malay advancement sustainable by generating more of it from within the community.

We already have the capacity to do so, but we need to empower the community to harness it. This will require a radical rethinking about the issues that have confronted our community for so long.

These challenges are elaborated on in this book: the emerging new politics, forging a people's economy, resolving the education question, the position of Islam in a multiracial society and the unravelling of the social fabric.

However, this paradigm shift should and in fact, can be done within the spirit of the Constitutional consensus that underpins this nation. We cannot and do not have to compromise on the Constitutional provisions on the status of the Malay Rulers, the position of Bahasa Malaysia as the National language, Islam as the religion of the Federation and the special position of the Malays. These provisions were guaranteed in the negotiations to achieve our Independence and should be maintained to reflect the historical context of Malaysia as a nation.

But just as we must not forget our past, so too must we face the challenges of the future. The future of the Malays cannot be separated from other Malaysians, and I will touch on this at the end of the book by exploring the idea of the 'Malaysian Dream'.

Some might then wonder why I am writing a book that seemingly addresses purely Malay concerns when the basic thrust of the book itself is towards accepting the reality of the Bangsa Malaysia. I would argue that this book is necessary given the fact that Malays have been indoctrinated to believe that any move towards the latter will result in them losing out.

Furthermore, as the Malays form the demographic majority, Malaysia as a whole cannot change if they do not see the necessity for this change. Achieving a Bangsa Malaysia is contingent upon shifting the discourse from Malay supremacy to that of Malay leadership.

What does this mean? To me, it represents a Malay community that is committed to expand opportunities for all Malaysians. My dream is for my people to be confident of their faith and their traditions, and at the same time value life in a multiracial society. I hope that my children and their children—indeed all Malaysian children—will one day live in a country that is home to all.

The Malays must show leadership and the non-Malays too must play their role to end the zero-sum game that has bogged us down for so long in order to achieve this. Malaysia can only succeed if its entire people comes together to make the national project work. The one reason that should compel us to do this is that it is simply the right thing to do.

I believe the Malays of the 21st century, especially the young, are ready for this. We have the confidence to face the future while continuing to hold on to our roots. Our country has achieved this much because earlier generations had the courage to make the right decisions. The burden is now on us.

A NEW POLITICAL PARADIGM

8 MARCH 2008: WHICH WAY FORWARD?

The General Elections held on 8 March 2008 shocked pundits and the public alike. The result—BN's second ever loss of its powerful two-third majority as well as the fall of four state governments in addition to PAS' retaining Kelantan—was beyond the expectation of most people. I managed to get 55.8 percent of the popular votes in the Seri Setia state constituency in Kelana Jaya, Selangor, and many others obtained even more impressive results!

Many commentators—including those who ignored the signs when the early results were announced on the evening of 8 March and pretended it was business as usual for BN—then changed their opinions as people debated, discussed and deliberated on the causes and effects of the shocking results.

UMNO had gone into the election fanning racial sentiments within the Malay community,[1] while PAS and Keadilan both reached out to the non-Malays, as did the DAP with the Malays. Although it was unsurprising that the Chinese and Indian minorities voted overwhelmingly against BN, it was significant that the Malays swung towards PR as well, albeit to a smaller extent.

Even then, urban Malays showed a shift closer to that of the non-Malay communities, indicating that they were willing to give the more moderate and consensual approach of what became the PR a chance.[2]

In actual numbers, the ranks of the Malay MPs increased from 123 in 2004 to 130. This dispels the notion that the 2008 General Election 'broke the power of the Malays' in any way.

Many factors, which we are all aware of, contributed to the result. The BN suffered from a weak leadership and in-fighting while costs of living and crime rates went up. Keadilan, led by the recently-released Datuk Seri Anwar Ibrahim, campaigned aggressively and struck an informal understanding with PAS and DAP, while the Malaysian blogosphere reached a critical mass and provided a powerful medium for discontent that avoided the country's media controls.

If some took 8 March as a freak result, the 2008 Permatang Pauh by-election in August emphasised the mood for change. Anwar's wife, Keadilan President Datuk Seri Dr Wan Azizah Wan Ismail stood down after nine years and three elections as MP, to make room for her husband.

Broadly speaking, the BN approached the by-election with the same strategy they had in March. Permatang Pauh is, after all, almost 70 percent Malay. Perhaps UMNO's strategists assumed even the Malays

---

1   The definition of Malay itself is a contentious subject. A Malay, as described in this book, generally refers to the legal definition provided in Article 160 of the Federal Constitution: "a person who professes Islam, habitually speaks the Malay language, and conforms to Malay custom and who has at least one ancestor from the Malay Peninsula or Singapore". However, in the case of the Malays prior to Independence, we will refer to them as an ethnic group. There has been debate between defining Malays as the specific ethnic group from Sumatra or as the broad Austronesian people inhabiting Southeast Asia including for example, the Javanese, the Bugis and the Minangkabau. A brief analysis can be found in Syed Husin Ali's *The Malays: Their Problems and Future* (Kuala Lumpur: The Other Press, 2008), while a more academic and broad perspective is provided by Barnard, Timothy P. (ed.), *Contesting Malayness: Malay Identity Across Boundaries* (Singapore: Singapore University Press, 2004).

2   Ong Kian Ming in 'Making Sense of the Political Tsunami', *Malaysiakini* 11 March 2008 estimated that the overall swing of Malay voters against BN was about 5 percent, compared to 30 percent for the Chinese and 35 percent for the Indians. But in the west coast of the peninsula, in particular urban areas, the Malay shift was greater. Ong pointed out that it would be impossible for seats like Balik Pulau, Gombak and Lembah Pantai to fall without a sizeable swing in the Malay vote. Furthermore, Kedah, a state in the Malay belt, also fell to PR with a swing of 12.7 percent.

who voted for the Opposition in March might have regrets due to the scale of the UMNO defeat and PR's persistent multiracial agenda. In addition, a new sodomy allegation had been made against Anwar, echoing the sacking in 1998. The accuser even swore on the Qu'ran the day before nomination day for added effect and this was broadcasted throughout the constituency during the entire campaign.

Yet, the people of Permatang Pauh rejected UMNO's dog-whistle politics. Anwar won with a 15,671 majority, bigger than his wife's 13,388 margin in March. Malays, especially young Malays, flocked overwhelmingly to vote for Anwar.

This result was further confirmed in Kuala Terengganu, where the UMNO incumbent MP passed away at the end of 2008. The by-election in a constituency where 88 percent of the voters were Malays was won by PAS candidate, Abdul Wahid Endut with over 2,500 votes over the BN candidate.

Some went as far as to claim that racial politics had come to an end. That is, perhaps, being overly optimistic. We only have to note the worry many Malays expressed, regardless of BN's scaremongering, in the period immediately after the elections to understand that race still matters.

A friend of mine from my college days happened to be a registered voter in my constituency and assisted my campaign. Not long after the elections, he met me in my constituency office.

"I managed to persuade my mother, an UMNO supporter to give you her vote this time around," he told me, "but now she's starting to get worried. She thinks that the big swing against BN is jeopardising the Malay interest."

At the same time, just as many were not too confident going into the elections; the euphoria and excitement generated after 8 March created a level of expectation that was unrealistic. Many wanted things to change overnight, while some saw the victory as a way to share the spoils of war and thus wanted more of the same to continue, only under a different name.

The challenge after 8 March was to manage these expectations and focus on the big picture. We need to continue delivering tangible changes while assuring existing players in the establishment that they still have a role to play. We need to convince the Malays that they will truly benefit from the new administration, contrary to what BN is making it out to be.

What seems certain, however, is that Malaysian politics will never be the same again. The results showed that the 21st century Malay was ready to listen to different ideas if political parties had the courage to make that argument and give more consideration to non-racial factors in their political calculation. The younger Malays, especially were more discerning. BN had vacated the political centre that was its strength in the past, and now PR is trying hard to fill that void. Only by seizing the position can Malays and Malaysians as a whole be driven forward.

The 8 March elections was truly a historic chapter in Malaysian politics that caught many Malaysians by surprise. Such an event could only have happened due to a range of factors all pointing to the same direction, something that probably takes place once or twice in a lifetime. What is important is that we ensure we grab the opportunities that emerge to push for change.

THE NEW POLITICS

What augurs well for the Malays and indeed all Malaysians is that our local politics is now more competitive with the emergence of the two-party system. The big-tent model of the Alliance Party that was inherited by the BN had previously proved to be a winning political machine to obtain the support of Malaysia's plural voters.

In the past, DAP and PAS could only win in seats where the non-Malays and Malays respectively made up a substantial majority. In fact, BN's strength lay in mixed-seats as Malays would not vote for DAP and non-Malays would not vote for PAS. With the emergence of Keadilan and Pakatan Rakyat, BN can no longer be complacent as the voters have matured.

At the same time, having thrown out BN after half a century of being in power, the voters would not hesitate to punish PR if we too, fail to deliver. No political party can afford to take the Malaysian public for granted anymore. Ultimately, 8 March was not so much a victory for PR as it was for the people as a whole.

To me, these developments showed that the 21st century Malay is ready to consider different ideas. While the older generation's perspective continues to be dominated by the BN's historical role in achieving Independence, instilling racial harmony and managing development in the past, younger Malays are holding BN responsible for failing to maintain ethnic relations and improve development.

They expect better.

Previously, this succeeded because the component parties played the race card at the grassroots but the coalition made provision for elite cooperation and a sense of national unity. Of late, however, it is apparent that the BN had vacated the political centre that was its strength in the past, and PR now is trying hard to fill that void and bring the nation to the next level. We feel that such a broad-based, non-sectarian approach is essential if Malaysians as a whole are to be driven forward politically.

Of course, UMNO's knee-jerk response to this development, where more Malay representatives have emerged from different parties, is to posit that Malays are becoming disunited. This, they argue, is a dilution of Malay political power. Nevermind the just-stated reality that the 2008 General Elections actually resulted in more Malay MPs being elected. UMNO has claimed that what is bad for the party is bad for the community. Period.

Yet, after half a century, UMNO's dominance of Malay support has become bad for both Malays and all Malaysians. Ordinary teachers and civil servants that made up UMNO's rank and file in the past have been replaced by contractors. In the past, members from all walks of life in UMNO sacrificed their wealth for the party's struggle. Today, totally unqualified opportunists become instant millionaires or gain influential government posts simply by virtue of holding positions in the party.

The party has become a vehicle of vested interests. This has resulted in the loss of connection of party members with the concerns of the ordinary Malays, let alone the non-Malays. It has come to a point where what UMNO members see as good for the party is no longer accepted as such by the public at large. In spite of all the rhetoric about Malay unity, the UMNO leaders themselves engage in bitter factional battles to satisfy their thirst for power. As has been oft-stated before, 'Melayu UMNO' no longer equals 'Melayu Malaysia'.

BN operated on the basis of divide and rule. UMNO represents the Malays, MCA the Chinese and MIC the Indians. From the top national leadership down to the grassroots community leaders, the problems of the people are compartmentalised according to the different races, to be solved by the respective parties. The experiences of 2008, with the myriad ethnic and governance problems coming to the fore, have shown that this modus operandi is no longer viable.

But the emergence of Pakatan Rakyat led by Keadilan has brought about a new approach in politics. The idea that the people are supreme has confounded the myth of *Ketuanan Melayu* promoted by BN; the idea that the problems of each community are for the country as a whole to solve, not merely for the community alone; and the idea that politics involves consultation and compromise—not command and control.

We also note the role of the new media in shaping new politics. Traditionally, BN's control over the divided media perpetuated its style of the old politics. But with the combination of Web 2.0 and the proliferation of mobile devices, this control has been undermined. The establishment can no longer dictate what the ordinary Malaysians voice out or talk about.

The young voters who many fear to be apathetic seem to be energised by these developments. It is important that they are continuously included in the political process to promote a sense of ownership for our democracy. A combination of more space for political participation and a discourse that reflects their concerns will go a long way towards securing their involvement.

Some Malays feel unnerved by the change. They are not used to the openness. Yet, while the Malays might not agree with all the opinions voiced out, they must have the confidence to argue and justify their views to a more discerning public. To tell people to shut up and stop is no longer an option. That is the reality, and we cannot turn back the clock.

This also means a shift from an obsession with narrow ideologies and sectarian politics towards the middle ground in search of common solutions to common problems, something that ought to apply to PR as well. In the days where the PR parties were the Opposition, they could afford to paint politics as a partisan battleground and offer impractical, if perhaps, idealistic solutions. But with the responsibility of government, the parties need to distinguish themselves from the BN on the basis of tangible and practical policies on the ground that reflect PR's vision for Malaysia.

We need to shift political discourse away from racial rhetoric to proper policies. We must provide the politics of hope, not play up the politics of fear. But old habits die hard and we see that BN has continued to rely on desperate and cynical tactics—like the second sodomy charge on Anwar, trumped-up corruption charges and of course, the blatantly unconstitutional overthrow of the Perak state government—to face the resurgent power of the people after 8 March, 2008. Gutter politics like this must be stopped to restore faith in our political institutions.

Ultimately, new politics mean relying less on personalities and empowering our institutions. A mature democracy should be able to experience stable political transitions as the institutions will continue to underpin the country regardless of which political party is in power. In effect, we need to get all Malaysians involved in the governance of the nation through vibrant institutions and a vocal civil society.

The old political culture distracted the Malays from thinking about the real issues that affect society. Too much talk has been about dominating the institutions, rather than having efficient and effective institutions that can realise the spirit of our Constitution as envisioned by our Founding Fathers.

There is no denying that there are particular issues that especially affect the Malay community more than others. Whether it is economic backwardness, social ills or the lack of academic achievement, the

Malays have more than their fair share of the statistics. It is unsurprising that Malays are worried by their community's predicament.

But in a plural country like Malaysia, it becomes more meaningful if we learn to talk about and with other communities. It is not wrong for Malays to be concerned and offended about an Indian teenager being killed in police custody. It is not wrong for an Indian to be concerned when a Chinese student is unable to get a place in university.

Like it or not, Malay political leadership, which while a reality considering the country's history and demographics, can only be sustained if it continues to be seen as just and fair to all that make up the people of this country. In this day and age, Malay leaders need to be able to articulate issues that affect all Malaysians. It simply makes more sense to. We are not 'less Malay' fighting for the rights of others—it makes us even more so. After all, aren't tolerance and hatred of oppression hallmarks of our culture and religion?

It is when our discourse moves beyond these narrow communal concerns and becomes one that empathises with the plight affecting other communities that we will know we have moved forward. While this silo mentality might be understandable to a certain extent, it does not reflect the realities of the Malaysian society where there is no such thing as a zero-sum game. We all depend on one another; it is difficult to separate the welfare of a single community from the others.

We are, after all, our brother's keepers. We all have a stake in this land. In the words of John Donne, "all mankind is of one author, and is one volume ... any man's death diminishes me, because I am involved in mankind". Any injustice against any Malaysian, regardless of his or her ethnicity or religion, diminishes our common citizenship and our common humanity. This, we must always keep in mind.

When Ali bin Abu Talib, the Prophet's nephew and the fourth Caliph of Islam was asked about a Muslim's relationship with a non-Muslim, he answered, *"Akhukum fil insaniah,"* or a brother in humanity.

Furthermore, the Malays need to wake up from the siege mentality of seeing everyone conspiring to keep them backwards. Similarly, the non-Malays need to stop seeing genuine moves to advance the national cause and national identity as insidious plots to destroy their cultural identities. It is attitudes like these that have constantly kept our people apart.

We need to start a public dialogue about building better schools, hospitals and public transport rather than about what this or that race gets. We need to deliberate more on strengthening competence, accountability and transparency. All this will benefit ordinary Malaysians in general and the Malays in particular. It is only when our campaigns debate about these fundamentals that we can say that our politics have matured.

At the end of the day, we need to empower the people and institutions to ensure that the new politics we fought hard for can be passed on to the next generation. We need to attract the brightest and most passionate Malaysians, regardless of race, to join politics to ensure that better policies are formulated for the society. We need to fight corruption and sleaze to restore a sense of respect for our political and public institutions. We need a political system based on respecting the dignity of man that will bring about greater respect and trust in its citizens.

WHY KEADILAN?

I had been involved with Keadilan since 2001 when I was just 19 years old, but only formally became a member in 2005. I am part of the new generation of Keadilan members who did not previously belong to any other political party or NGO. Back then, Keadilan had a single Parliamentary seat after the Opposition's rout in 2004. While Datuk Seri Anwar Ibrahim's release from prison rejuvenated the party to a certain extent, many continued and to an extent still continue to ask: What is Keadilan's objective? Why did I join Keadilan? Why not UMNO or PAS?

I have always had an interest in politics for as long as I can remember. As a Muslim, I believe that I have a responsibility to make a difference in society, and I felt that politics was the best avenue for me to do so. Also, my faith was an important consideration. Racism has no place in Islam. It was this tenet, among other things, that led to Islam's remarkable development in its earliest years over 1,400 years ago.

When the *Reformasi* movement emerged in 1998, I was 16 years old. Like many young Malaysians in those dark days, I was swept away by the movement and the Parti Keadilan Nasional that was born as a result. My sense of decency and justice was outraged by the gross human rights abuses of that period, which continue to this day.

I felt that Malaysians had to stand up and be counted. While the sacking of Datuk Seri Anwar Ibrahim ignited the movement, I was inspired by the values and vision that Anwar articulated and the struggle against the oppressive state that he had fought.

In 2001, I began writing commentaries on various websites, and soon issues such as a needs-based affirmative action and the end of racial politics became my regular subjects. Even then, I felt that this was the logical extension of the *Reformasi*. I contended that the Malay mentality was changing.

Keadilan, I believe, is the heir to a long legacy in Malaysian politics. Since the end of the Second World War, a group of Malays accepted the country's plural nature and the need for multiracial political support. This came about with the AMCJA-PUTERA coalition and later, the Alliance Party and eventually Merdeka in 1957. The IMP, Gerakan and Tan Sri Tan Chee Khoon's short-lived Parti Keadilan Masyarakat all attempted to bring about this cooperation to the next level—namely a single, multiracial party with Malay leadership. But these efforts either failed or were diluted by the *realpolitik* of communal chauvinism.

By establishing a multiracial party that reflects Malaysia, Keadilan fosters a greater sense of trust between the different communities. Keadilan's linkage to the progressive movement was strengthened through its merger with the Parti Rakyat Malaysia, bringing into the former a rich tradition of progressive nationalism.

Keadilan's multiracial approach allows for far-reaching changes to be introduced. This will, hopefully, tone down the racial rhetoric, therefore promoting greater understanding and acceptance among Malaysians. It is time to advance a truly Malaysian agenda.

In the past, each community saw politics as a battle where one community gains and the others lose. This was unhealthy for the Malays, for while they were given a sense of security through the ideal of *Ketuanan Melayu* (Malay Lordship or supremacy), it had become more of a smokescreen to perpetuate corruption and stifle dissent amongst the existing political elite that was detrimental to many ordinary Malays.

Without a Malay-led multiracial party, the Opposition would be split across the political spectrum—DAP for the Chinese and Indians while PAS was limited to the Malays. Without a party in the middle to hold them together, they could not possibly combine forces to stand up to BN. With the arrival of Keadilan, Malaysia's Opposition parties could truly portray themselves as a government-in-waiting that could match BN's broad spectrum of support.

One must not, however, forget or devalue the countless sacrifices that the veteran leaders of DAP and PAS rendered to their nation in standing up to the brute force of the BN for the sake of the people. They are truly Malaysian heroes and Keadilan honours their tireless efforts in bringing true democracy to the nation.

Many have asked what our party's ideology is. Some see us as just a vehicle for Anwar's political ambitions. Nothing could be further from the truth. Keadilan's ideology is framed by 17 core principles, the first of which is to build "a society that is just and a nation that is democratic, progressive and united". In practice, Keadilan is a broad-based coalition built on the radical centre.

Given the great diversity of cultures and political beliefs in Malaysia, it is only natural that we do not focus on a narrow ideology. Of course, some people will always question the viability of the Keadilan's coalition-model, both internally and in the context of Pakatan Rakyat. They ask again and again: how are we different from the BN?

It cannot be denied that Keadilan has had its share of problems. It is true that we have a long way to go and a lot to prove. But here is the crucial difference: while UMNO and BN rely on elite power and is suspicious of democracy, Keadilan and Pakatan are empowered by it.

BN was a marriage of convenience by the most powerful and most selfish elements in Malaysia at the time. Pakatan Rakyat was a band of activists united by a common scar: we had all, at some point in our lives, been disgusted by or suffered under the oppressive force of the government under the BN.

Even a cursory reading will demonstrate how many successful and groundbreaking political movements were built on broad coalitions focused on immediate issues and core principles without being bound in ideological straightjackets. In the long run, a nationally successful political party has to represent the spectrum of the society it represents.

President Franklin Delano Roosevelt managed to bring about far-reaching reforms in American politics by bringing together liberals, left-leaning unionists, minorities and conservative Southern Democrats that broadly supported the New Deal and the advent of the Second World War helped to secure his four electoral victories. Ronald Reagan, on the other hand, gained support from Southern Democrats, evangelical Christians, neo-liberals as well as old-fashioned liberal Republicans. Even earlier still, Abraham Lincoln united his 'Team of Rivals' into a Cabinet that won the American Civil War and ended slavery there. New Labour was established to provide a more inclusive social democratic agenda beyond the ideologically coherent but electorally disastrous Old Labour ideology.

In the Malaysian context, the Alliance and BN initially worked because it pursued a 'big tent strategy'. BN was more the big tent than the Alliance as it consisted of political parties ranging from the communal to the liberal, from the socialist to the nationalist. It was formed following the 13 May 1969 riots and now enjoys all the benefits of incumbency. Even PAS was part of the coalition in the 1970s.

Yet, this is still essentially a coalition of race-based parties, and that is where things went horribly wrong for the country. The downside is that beyond the coalition, the component parties still play the politics of divide and rule, rousing their constituencies with the politics of fear and prejudice. This does not augur well for national unity. Keadilan is a step beyond this in that it tries to bring the conversation to the grassroots, to allow Malaysians to grasp the complexity and challenges of living in a plural society.

Keadilan's vision—among others, to promote respect for the

constitutional monarchy while strengthening parliamentary democracy; to establish and promote the rule of law, the independence of the media and judiciary; to uphold Islam as the religion of the Federation while guaranteeing the rights of non-Muslims the freedom of worship and conscience; to shape a dynamic and fair economy that values growth and distribution—is the right way forward for Malaysians in the 21st century.

As I mentioned earlier, Keadilan, as the youngest of the PR parties, faces many challenges—the need to get better candidates, to build deeper grassroots and to create a more coherent organisation. Post-8 March, some of these weaknesses became apparent as the excitement and euphoria faded.

But the party is a reflection of society. Prior to the 12th General Elections, many did not give the party any chance. Even within our own members, many potential candidates who were identified chose not to run as it was seen as merely a waste of time, money and effort: you invest so much of all three only to lose.

As many either worked in the public sector, GLCs or in private companies that have dealings with the government, not many were willing to take the risk. Partly, that explained why a 26-year-old like me was given the chance to run in the elections.

Like our candidates, we are a young party and our enthusiasm, as well as idealism, sustain us. We may make mistakes, but like all right-minded young people, we learn from them and become stronger as a result. We do not expect Malaysians to excuse us for our faults or demand anything less than the highest standards from us, but we do hope they understand that all political parties have their ups and downs. We will do our best for them in either case.

But with a large number of very young leaders unburdened by our troubled political past, we can turn these uncertain times into an opportunity to establish Keadilan as a viable political party that truly represents Bangsa Malaysia and a meaningful change for the country. Everyone likes winners, and where members now come in the thousands unlike previously, we need to ensure that Keadilan's and PR's original vision as well as the blood, sweat and tears shed by the reformists who founded them remain cherished by every member.

TOWARDS A PEOPLE'S ECONOMY

THE NEP: A RECONSIDERATION

In 2001, I wrote in *Malaysiakini*:

> ... Once our cosmetically-impressive economy faltered, and with the increasing momentum of Opposition pressure following the sacking of the deputy prime minister, the Malaysian people, and the Malays in particular, are realising the failure of the NEP ...
>
> Most of the Malays are now aware that the real threat to Malay progress may not necessarily come from the non-Malays, but possibly from the rich Malays themselves, the only real beneficiaries of the NEP.

It was at this time that race became a regular topic of conversation between my father and I, and I began to think critically about the NEP. This issue has always loomed heavily in my intellectual history, as it is closely tied to my own family's story.

My father, who was born in 1930 in Kota Bharu, Kelantan, came from a family of modest means, although he could count palace scribes and Muslim scholars among his ancestors. His father was a religious teacher for the police.

My father started his education in an Arab school, called the Islah

School, in the middle of the Japanese Occupation of Malaya during the Second World War. In this, he was following the footsteps of his father, grandfather and great-grandfather, but his family could not afford the final step of sending him to the Middle East to complete his education. Instead, they allowed him to 'lie' about his age to ensure that he would be eligible to attend the only English school in Kota Bharu at that time, the Sultan Ismail College.

My father did well there, one of the many Malays to benefit from an English education. He ended up in Victoria School, Singapore and stayed at the residence of Mansor Adabi's family, who is known to history as the erstwhile husband of Natrah Maarof @ Maria Hertogh, she of that huge controversy in the early 1950s. Later, my father was among a small number of Malays who managed to get a place in University Malaya, which was then in Singapore, to read History. Upon graduating in 1958, he joined the civil service of the newly-independent Malaya.

But while my father was part of a select group of Malays who succeeded at that time, many more were left behind. The plight went unresolved for a decade after Independence, angering many of the Malay Young Turks.[3] They clamoured for far-reaching measures to uplift the Malays.

These undercurrents, stirred by the 1969 General Elections, exploded into the racial riots on 13 May and the Young Turks took it as an opportunity to oust Tunku Abdul Rahman from office. Having secured power, they then implemented a raft of policies that eventually became known as the NEP under the tireless leadership of Tun Abdul Razak Hussein.

My father welcomed the NEP and as a civil servant, was at the

---

3 'The Young Turks' was a term used to describe the educated young Malays in UMNO who were dissatisfied with the old guard in UMNO in the 1960s. This included Mahathir Mohamad, Musa Hitam and Tengku Razaleigh Hamzah, who pushed for aggressive economic measures and gained prominence with the implementation of the NEP.

front line of its implementation. As he was at the Public Services Department, my father travelled across the world to seek university places for Malaysians who had received extensive government scholarships for tertiary education. Given that many of the recipients of the scholarship were Malays, my father earned a reputation as an honest and passionate fighter for the Malay cause, doing all he could to expand the opportunities of the Malay community.[4] My father retired in 1988, two years before the NEP was supposed to end. It formally did, but its ideals and objectives were perpetuated under a different name, while its abuse and misuse began to grow much to his unease.

The excesses of *Operasi Lalang* and the Judicial Crisis of 1987 probably made him further disillusioned with the government. Tuan Guru Nik Aziz Nik Mat visited our home just prior to his retirement and offered him a spot in the PAS' slate of candidates for Kelantan. PAS, as we know, eventually took power there under Nik Aziz's leadership. Nik Aziz hoped to recruit a man who understood the workings of government. My father was keen, but my mother did not want him to have anything to do with politics. As a result, he was content to take a few advisory positions and was put on the board of a GLC-scholarship foundation, in recognition of his role in expanding the scholarship policy. This was the typical path of a senior civil servant pensioner.

Ten years later, the *Reformasi* erupted. At that time, both my parents (including my previously apolitical mother) flocked to the movement, even before I was truly convinced. My father stopped buying *The New Straits Times* out of disgust and faithfully attended various Opposition programmes. Being a pensioner who had passed his opportunity to enter politics, it was left to his young brothers and eventually me to be active participants in the movement. We, in a sense, accomplished what he could not.

---

4   There was a joke, however, that while the Chinese said my father favoured the Malays, the Malays in turn accused my father of favouring the Kelantanese!

I remember that it was at this point of time, as I was grappling with what the *Reformasi* meant to me, that I began debating with my father on the NEP. These little talks were all the more interesting because the generation gap between us was wider than most fathers and sons, particularly in terms of our eras, backgrounds and upbringing. As a brash young man then and fiercely idealistic, I believed that the policy was wrong—both from the Islamic and social justice perspectives—in that it focused on race, instead of needs.

My father, coming from a different worldview, engaged me in conversation on why he and his generation felt that the policy was necessary. Although we had our differences, both of us eventually came round to the realisation that the NEP had played its role but as it currently stands, is unsustainable.

In fact, while the UMNO Youth continues to focus on the issue of corporate equity, we tend to overlook the NEP's greatest success, which was the creation of a Malay middle class. We could and should be proud of that. But it is indeed a tragedy when the children of the NEP continue to believe, and continue to promote the belief, that Malays will forever need these 'crutches' to succeed. The NEP was created not for the beneficiaries' own children to continue being beneficiaries, but so that *they could hold their own*. That is the only way we can sustain and eventually improve on our previous achievements. Yet, we have certain UMNO Youth leaders trumpeting the need to defend the 30 percent equity policy when this only benefits certain Malay elites while the basic problems of the Malay community remain unresolved.

My father would watch in horror at how the debate on the NEP continued to develop in a way that he did not envision it would when they were working on its blueprint 30 years ago. These young post-NEP UMNO leaders often take the NEP for granted, thinking that the one way forward is to cling to it forever. The most vocal Malays are not the self-confident, hardworking Malays he dreamed of, but populist demagogues. The dangers are further multiplied by the fact that many are now educated in a system that no longer promotes free inquiry and critical thinking, unlike the architects of the NEP.

And the consequences of this are dire. Malays who question the need for the NEP are now branded as 'traitors' to their race. The NEP has simply become twisted from its original objectives and is now monstrous. What was once a noble government initiative to change the lives of millions for the better has now, unfortunately, become a point of division and acrimony. I am certain that the founding fathers of the NEP would not approve of how it what it has become today. Let us not forget that one of the policy's original goals was to eradicate poverty amongst all Malaysians regardless of their ethnicity—and that should continue to be our goal with or without the NEP.

I was thus pleased, when I joined Keadilan in 2005, that Datuk Seri Anwar Ibrahim made a drastic announcement that he would seek to move the Malaysian economy beyond the NEP. Even then, as Anwar would confide later, many Malay leaders in the party (as well as a handful of Malay and even non-Malay friends) advised him against the move. But he was convinced that while it might be unpopular among the Malays, it was necessary—not to win the support of the non-Malays, but for the Malays themselves.

Later (when I was working for him), Anwar prepared a crucial document which was distributed across the country to introduce Keadilan's Malaysian Economic Agenda. Essentially it advocated an economy focused on growth and affirmative action regardless of race.

In 1970, Malays accounted for 74 percent of poor households in the country. At RM172, the mean Malay household income was less than half of the mean household income of the Chinese.[5] The Young Turks blamed then Prime Minister Tunku Abdul Rahman for failing to build Malay economic clout by continuing *laissez-faire* economic policies.

---

5   Government of Malaysia, Third Malaysia Plan 1976–1980 pp. 179, 72–74.

The NEP was thus launched in the Second Malaysia Plan in 1971:

> (The NEP) incorporates the two-pronged objective of eradicating poverty, irrespective of race and restructuring Malaysian society to reduce and eventually eliminate the identification of race with economic functions ... (the government) will spare no efforts to promote national unity and develop a just and progressive Malaysian society in a rapidly expanding economy so that no one will experience any loss or feel any sense of deprivation of his rights, privileges, income, job and opportunity ... To achieve our overall objective of national unity, Malaysia needs more than merely a high rate of economic growth. While devoting our efforts to the task of achieving rapid economic development, we need to ensure at the same time that there is social justice, equitable sharing of income growth and increasing opportunities for employment ... . The Plan must succeed as it is vital to our survival as a happy and united nation.

Hence, following the implementation of the NEP, UMNO sought to gain control of all the economic levers within the government. The extension of the three-party Alliance to BN allowed UMNO to flex its muscles as the position of MCA and MIC in the coalition was diluted. Furthermore, the emergence of consensual politics with the 'big-tent' coalition of BN as well as the neutralisation of politically contentious racial issues through the Sedition Act provided much-needed cover for the Young Turks to push their agenda through.

A prominent aspect of the NEP was the 30 percent equity target, which was implemented via the Industrial Coordination Act 1975. The objective was for Malay individuals to own 30 percent of corporate equity. In 1970, the Malays were holding only to 2.4 percent of corporate equity.⁶ To follow through this plan, Yayasan Pelaburan Bumiputera was set up in 1978. Through PNB, the Yayasan became a trustee for shares allocated to the Bumiputeras through the Industrial Coordination Act. The Bumiputeras were given access to these shares through a novel unit trust fund, Amanah Saham Nasional through which individual Bumiputeras could invest in shares by way of small investments of as low as a few ringgit.

Another key feature of the NEP was the BCIC, which promoted participation among the Bumiputeras in the economy. In practice, this translated to 30 percent equity quota for Bumiputera firms for construction projects, as well as a price discount, usually to the tune of 10 percent, for Bumiputera businessmen.

Nevertheless, it is also important to note that while the government advocated radical economic restructuring, it undertook to do so in the context of a growing economy. Tun Razak noted from the beginning that the effort to improve the economic well-being of the Malays should not be done at the expense of the non-Malays.

One of the ways the government sought to realise this aim was by focusing on reducing foreign equity ownership, rather than the equity ownership of other non-Malay citizens. In 1970, foreigners owned 63.4 percent of corporate equity in the country, while non-Malay citizens owned 28.3 percent. Fifteen years later, the figures were 26.0 percent and 47.7 percent respectively, while for the Bumiputera, the percentage grew from 2.4 percent to 19.1 percent in the same period.⁷

The newfound confidence of the young nation was epitomised in the Dawn Raid in 1981 when PERNAS acquired Guthrie at the London Stock Exchange without the latter's knowledge. Soon, other foreign companies operating in the country were also acquired. Tan Sri Dato'

---

6   Leete, Richard. *Malaysia: From Kampung to Twin Towers* (Shah Alam: Oxford Fajar, 2007), p. 162.

7   Ibid.

Abdul Khalid Ibrahim, the current Menteri Besar of Selangor, played a major part by virtue of his position in PNB at the time.

To further ease the pressure on the non-Malays, the government tried to increase foreign investment. Active effort was made to attract electronic firms through the creation of free-trade zones. This allowed the economy to grow and to a certain extent, freed the non-Malays from the pressure of restructuring, while at the same time providing many young Malays industrial employment on a large scale.

When Tun Dr Mahathir Mohamad took over in 1981, the NEP's emphasis shifted. Through his Malaysia Inc. policy, the government embarked on a privatisation exercise in tandem with the values espoused by Margaret Thatcher in Britain and Ronald Reagan in America. Privatisation, which was announced two years after Mahathir took over, provided the avenue for the Prime Minister to create Malay capitalists.

If the NEP's focus in its early years was on the creation of state institutions and Malay capacity-building through education and training, Mahathir wanted to create instant Malay tycoons, who could then bring more Malay firms into the supply chain. Central to this exercise was Tun Daim Zainuddin, a lawyer-turned-businessman-turned-politician.

Privatisation was done in many ways. One way was the outright sale of government assets to the public, for instance the sale of utility companies like Tenaga Nasional Berhad and Telekom Malaysia, although the government continued to maintain a substantial stake in these companies. Another way was through the award of concessions of infrastructure projects such as highways, power producers and the like to privatised parties, for example the North-South Highway, otherwise known as the build-manage or build-manage-transfer methods. Thirdly, many support services to government bodies were outsourced to different contractors although the main body remained in the government's hands.

Another pet project of Mahathir was heavy industries. This included the establishment of HICOM in 1982 which led to the national car project, Proton. Proton produced its first model, Saga in 1985. One of the objectives of the project was to build a Bumiputera supply chain for the industry in order to gradually reduce our reliance on Japanese parts over the years.

Mahathir was known as a man in a hurry. This led to a no-nonsense attitude obsessed with immediate results. Indeed, privatisation was seen as a way to hasten the attainment of the objectives of the NEP. While his urgency allowed the country to achieve an accelerated level of development, it also led to short cuts with many unintended consequences: the weakening of state institutions vis-à-vis the political elite, the spread of corruption and a deterioration of the rule of law.

This was his great contradiction. While he often spoke out against the Malay's reliance on the state, he could not break away from the fact that his party's power was based on this relationship. The net result of his 'privatisations' was always the arrogation of power to the executive and the uncontrolled growth of the state.

Hence, it was unsurprising that the opaque privatisation process resulted in many of the companies failing. Some struggled to make profits. Others, while remaining profitable, failed to provide the much vaunted improvement in services that was supposed to be the result of privatisation. The government had to step in to bail out the companies. Ironically, this meant that when the companies were profitable, the private parties reaped the rewards, but when they started to make losses, the government used taxpayers' money to come to their rescue. In short, profits were privatised but losses were nationalised. This was renationalisation, an admission that Mahathir's privatisation had failed.

Up to this day, the same pre-NEP challenges continue to bedevil the Malay community, though perhaps to a lesser extent. Malays still need to catch up in businesses, especially in the small- and medium-sized industries. Discrimination against the Malays in those sectors still exists and Malays still form the bulk of the rural and urban poor. There also needs to be urgent action to improve the performance of Malay students in schools and universities.[8]

On the other hand, many non-Malays benefited from the NEP as well. First, the social stability that emerged following the NEP was crucial in maintaining Malaysia's development until the 1990s, allowing non-Malays the space to prosper. Secondly, many of the non-Malay tycoons associated with the Malay political elite were given generous concessions and exemptions. Thirdly, certain elite non-Malay entrepreneurs benefited from 'Ali-Baba' deals whereby they appointed Malay partners and agents to get contracts.

One of the policies of the NEP was the awarding of APs by the Ministry of International Trade and Industry. APs are permits to sell foreign cars in the local market. The APs are given only to selected parties, who in turn, sell them to auto distributors for a hefty price. AP recipients or 'AP Kings' as they are known, are estimated to receive about RM1 billion a year! In fact, in 2005, when Tun Dr Mahathir started questioning the distribution of APs ostensibly to protect Proton, it was announced that about 20 companies control more than 50,000 APs!

UMNO claims that direct negotiations and APs are awarded for the benefit of the Malays. But surely a better system would be a Malay-only tender or a Malay-only competitive bidding for APs? This makes more sense than the alternative murky and questionable process. Indeed, the current approach only results in corruption that does not benefit ordinary Malays or foster greater long-run competitiveness among Malay entrepreneurs.

---

8   According to the *Ninth Malaysia Plan 2006–2010*, in 2004, 8.3 percent Bumiputera remain in overall poverty, as opposed to 0.6 percent Chinese and 2.9 percent Indian. The mean Bumiputera income in 2004 was RM2,711 as opposed to the national average of RM3,249. Ownership of share capital in 2004 was 18.9 percent.

Under Datuk Seri Abdullah Ahmad Badawi's administration, the government admitted that the NEP had failed to achieve many of its targets due to what they termed 'leakages'. Whether it is called leakages or corruption, its endemic nature in the country remains. In 2004, Morgan Stanley estimated that corruption over a two-decade period from the mid-1980s had cost Malaysia over US$100 billion! Even the government-mandated Special Task Force to Facilitate Businesses (PEMUDAH) in 2008 had estimated that about RM10 billion is lost annually from the gross domestic growth due to corruption.

We must replace policies that perpetuate rent-seeking with genuine capacity-building programmes that focus on expanding opportunities for all. Protectionist policies allow many Asian infant industries to grow but without removing the barriers, the industries will become inefficient and complacent, unable to compete with players from across the globe.

Similarly, while affirmative action can be justified for the worst-off in society, a perpetuation of the policy as certain individuals climb up the ladder while still being dependent on it risks making them uncompetitive in an increasingly globalised world. The unintended consequence of any interventionist policy is that it is difficult to wean anyone from a state of dependency.

Since the Malays make up the bulk of the poor, they will continue to benefit from a system that is focused on assisting those left behind. At the same time, this will ensure that the Malays who should be competing with other Malaysians—the middle classes—will do so. Currently, only a handful monopolise the benefits from the system allowing those at the bottom of the ladder to enjoy only the trickle-down benefits, thus accentuating the gap between the rich and poor within the Malay community.

We must also recognise that while many aspects of the NEP were designed to cope with the Malays generally existing in a rural society, the Malays today are far more urbanised. Urban, rather than rural poverty has emerged as the biggest challenge for the Malay community and Malaysia in general.

Non-racial affirmative action will promote social mobility. As a top Malay corporate leader once told me, when we talk about social mobility, we always refer to people at the bottom of the social ladder rising up. We forget that in such a scenario, those who are uncompetitive should also go down.

In other words, those who should have benefited from the NEP —the urban poor, the farmers, the fishermen—will be better off under such non-racial affirmative action rather than the one we have today. Of course, those who survive on cozy contracts and political connections will be forced to buck up, but the community and country will be better off. In short, the dignity of the Malays who can compete and the non-Malays who deserve assistance will be preserved under such an approach.

There are two potential arguments against this move. First, that Malays generally still lag behind and require assistance to compete. But in a policy where *Malaysians* who deserve help are aided, obviously all deserving Malays will get the help they need. They will inevitably benefit due to our nation's demographics, where they are a clear majority. Such a policy will free up much more resources to the Malays who truly and really need help.

Furthermore, damning Malays who can and should compete on a level playing field with other races to still require crutches to succeed is an admission that no matter how far they have improved socio-economically, they are still unable to compete on their own, whether these fault-lines are real or perceived. This implies that Malays are genetically inferior. Many Malays including those overseas—even in Singapore where the community feels it faces various forms of discrimination—have been able to succeed. Given the same opportunities, there is nothing to stop Malays from achieving as much as other communities. The second argument against non-racial affirmative action is that Malays require affirmative action regardless of need, but on the basis of their race alone. I accept that the historical position of the Malays and the other Bumiputeras should be acknowledged as enshrined in the Federal Constitution, but to extend it to far-reaching affirmative action based on race is contradictory to the essential principle of equality.

How can we then complain about discrimination against minorities in the West if we do not accord the same respect to other people in our country? There must be moral consistency to our stand. Preaching human rights when we are minorities but ignoring them when we are politically powerful reeks of hypocrisy. There are many Malays who are more recent migrants to the country compared to some Chinese and Indian families. On what basis should they be accorded preferential treatment?

I visited Singapore in 2008 and met the committee members of the Mendaki Club, where Malay professionals volunteer in programmes to uplift the Malay-Muslim community. One of those who was there was Nur Dianah Suhaimi, a *Straits Times* journalist whose essay 'Feeling Like the Least Favourite Child' caused a stir in bringing to the fore the feelings of many Malays on the island.

Singaporean Malays face real challenges in the form of dilution of political power, the elite bias as well as the perception of an inherent cultural deficit.[9] In Malaysia, they have always been used as a bogey of what would happen to the Malaysian Malays if the preferential policies are dismantled.

The feedback they gave was interesting. One opined that discrimination does exist against the Malays, and any achievement is looked upon by other Singaporeans merely as token achievements *granted* to the Malay community, not *attained* through their own effort

---

9   Lily Zubaidah Rahim provides the best analysis on the challenges facing the Singaporean Malay community in *The Singapore Dilemma: The Political and Educational Marginality of the Malay Community* (Shah Alam: Oxford University Press, 1998).

and merit. But one of them saw the lack of preferential policies and even the sense of discrimination as a badge of honour of the local Malay community as Malays have to succeed on their own. Ironically, reflecting on the plight of the non-Malays in Malaysia, they felt that they had to work twice as hard as the other Singaporeans in order to succeed, thus strengthening their resilience. As Nur Dianah wrote in her famous essay:

> Throughout my life, my father has always told me that as a Malay, I need to work twice as hard to prove my worth. He said people have the misconception that all Malays are inherently lazy.

Another possible argument is against the idea of affirmative action itself, regardless of socio-economic background or race being its basis. There are inherent problems with means-testing or targeting. Many who are uncomfortable with government intervention are fearful of 'social engineering'. Nobel laureate, Amartya Sen has listed the almost endless problems associated with this: information distortion; disutility and stigma; administrative costs, invasive loss and corruption; and the need for political sustainability and quality.

That these problems exist is undeniable. Means-testing requires the authorities to determine the income of the individual, and there are bound to be inaccuracies, intentional or otherwise, in determining the exact figure. This also opens the door to corruption due to the unequal bargaining power between the bureaucrats who administer means-testing and the applicants. There is also the issue of whether recipients would lose the incentive to earn more when doing so would mean them forfeiting their benefits.

The bottom line, however, is that we encounter these problems anyway in the current race-based affirmative action. There are communities at the margin of the Bumiputera categorisation: Indian and Chinese

Muslims, those from Thai, Portuguese and Peranakan ancestry as well as mixed-blood Bumiputeras who sometimes benefit as Bumiputeras and/or Malays and who sometimes do not. Often, it is the government official at the front desk who decides who gets what. The process therefore becomes a 'lottery' of sorts, albeit one with very few winners.

I also believe that while there are bound to be inconsistencies and costs attached to administering a means-based affirmative action, there are sufficient reasons for the government to intervene and play a role in helping all those who are the worst-off in society to succeed. It is crucial for the social fabric for the poor to be given room to fulfil their potential. Otherwise, marginalisation and 'ghettoisation' jeopardises society and the democratic system, leaving room for extremists to prosper and even threaten the survival of the state itself. This outweighs the potential drawbacks of the unintended consequences. Compared to a race-based system, a means-based system of affirmative action is far more superior.

Beyond that, in practical terms, what can be done to empower the Malay economy post-NEP?

First, I agree that bodies such as MARA and Tabung Haji should be retained as a trust for Malay advancement and progress. Ultimately, however, this should be handed over to the Malay community to administer for the benefit of the community at large. MARA can work with successful Malay corporate leaders and entrepreneurs to build a fund to invest in budding Malay entrepreneurs. This will create a sense of community solidarity and allow new entrants to understand the problems and issues affecting the Malay business community.

It will make the Malays less reliant on the government, and allow those who have succeeded to give back to society. This fund can take the form of academic and vocational scholarships, research grants and low-interest loans. MARA should play a more aggressive role in building Malay entrepreneurs, allowing Malay entrepreneurs to enter into various stages of the supply chain. At the bottom of the ladder, for the poorest among the community who would like to go into business, there can be collaboration with Muslim authorities for the utilisation of *zakat*. It is better for *zakat* to be used for sustainable capacity-building programmes rather than simple hand-outs that do not help Muslims to progress. The Singaporean Mendaki Fund is a good example of a community self-help programme.

It must be noted, however, that without a strong affirmative action policy to address the needs of the worst-off, community self-help programmes face the challenge of having the smallest pool of funds to help the most marginalised community. As Lily Zubaidah Rahim pointed out in *The Singapore Dilemma*, "The ethnic-based self-help paradigm is also likely to maintain the inter-ethnic socio-economic disparity due to the unequal material and political resources available to the different ethnic communities." But I believe the political clout of the Malays as well as the track record of these funds can be key components towards empowering the Malays in Malaysia.

Secondly, such funds could also be utilised to become a purchaser of last resort for Bumiputera assets. Currently, there are requirements for property quotas as well as exclusive Malay reserve lands. Furthermore, there also exist in certain states blanket initial rejections of any sale of Malay real estate to non-Malays. While the intention is to safeguard Malay access to real estate, it also penalises the Malays who purchase these properties from turning real property into liquidity. It is difficult to promote Malay participation in real estate through blanket rejections. The quotas might be justified on grounds of promoting diversity (interestingly, Singapore, where meritocracy supposedly reigns, also has racial quotas for Housing Development Board flats), although even that is debatable. By pooling funds to create a purchaser of last resort, Malays who are unable to find buyers for their property can still cash in on their property by selling it to the trust fund. At the same time, the trust fund can provide a discount for other Malay purchasers to purchase property.

Thirdly, the government should promote genuine inter-racial business partnerships, not the Ali-Baba kind where the Malay partner's only role is to obtain government contracts and licences while the real business is run by the non-Malay partner. All partners should contribute productively to the enterprise, leveraging on their respective strengths and networks. The growth of these partnerships will augur well for greater Malay confidence in gaining entry into business on a productive, non rent-seeking manner and will enhance inter-racial relationships and national integration. This is already happening as qualified Malays are no longer satisfied just being rent-seeking partners and demand equally productive roles in the partnership. The government needs, however, to actively encourage such developments. In 1998, according to the report for the Ninth Malaysia Plan to the government by the Centre for Public Policy Studies director Dr Lim Teck Ghee titled 'Corporate Equity Distributions: Past Trends and Future Policy', 29 percent of companies listed in Bursa Malaysia were Chinese-Malay partnerships. According to Dr Lim, these were genuine co-operations, not Ali-Baba partnerships:

> ... This new professional and entrepreneurial Bumiputera community is on par with non-Bumiputera in terms of competence and capacity to compete.
>
> The now wealthier and educated Bumiputera middle class is also emerging as a new entrepreneurial community, playing a prominent role in the development of new enterprises. A number of these new enterprises involving Bumiputera are based on partnerships with non-Bumiputera. These business ties that are becoming increasingly inter-ethnic in nature have been established on the basis of equal competency among the partners, with both contributing to the productive development of the firm.

The bottom line is that mechanisms such as quotas for Bumiputera shares or land are only short-term solutions that do not solve the issue of the community's weakness in the commercial sector. Instead, many of these solutions have paved the way for excesses and corruption to take root. Instead of capacity-building, we have been engrossed with rent-seeking. Our focus must be on improving our education system, uplifting the worst-off in society and empowering the Malay entrepreneurs in order to comprehensively and sustainably improve the economic development of the Malay community.

In a multiracial society such as Malaysia, it is impossible for any community to flourish while the rest suffer. While relative performance does matter, the focus must be towards creating a conducive and viable economic environment for all communities to prosper. The end goal is for each community to play its role for all Malaysians to succeed. This might sound a tad idealistic, but as a nation with a common destiny, there is no other way if Malaysia is to thrive.

It must be noted that my arguments look towards gradual and tangible changes, rather than allowing a 'free-for-all' by dismantling everything all at once. But there must be definite timelines and quantifiable objectives to measure the changes.

THE GLCS, MALAYS AND BUSINESS

After I returned from Britain in 2005, I spent nearly a year working at the GLC that sponsored my studies. Like most of their scholars, I was assigned to its management trainee programme and was later sent to its legal department. By June 2006, however, I had resigned to work for Datuk Seri Anwar Ibrahim and eventually paid off my bond.

I had, therefore, worked there for less than a year, but it did give me some insights into the nature of Malaysia's GLCs. The GLCs have, of course, come under intense scrutiny of late, very much a part of the larger debate over Malay participation in the nation's economic scenario.

Like many young professionals, my colleagues and I were often frustrated over the ethos of the GLC, especially its bureaucracy, inertia and obsession with hierarchy. Admittedly, these are the sorts of complaints that all young employees make against their organisations, but I think these problems are particularly serious in Malaysian GLCs.

Like almost every other national institution, they have become identified with a particular ethnic group (my own) and again, this has been a mixed blessing to the community as a whole. There have been many success stories—Petronas for one, is an example of what a GLC can achieve with less political interference and professional management. While it cannot be denied that GLCs have played a major role in creating a Malay middle class, the fact remains that our participation in the nation's economy, still bound to government activism rather than individual initiative, leaves much to be desired.

Nevertheless, the very fact that the GLCs have supposedly become so essential to the economic fortunes of a race makes any objective analysis of these institutions a difficult proposition. Again, this situation exists mainly to benefit the Malay political elite. The controversy over Dr Lim Teck Ghee's study, which I quoted earlier, is a case in point.

A year after I left the GLC, Dr Lim's study was published in which he acknowledged that the Malays have made substantial and significant progress since the introduction of the NEP. Among other things, he calculated that Malay equity surpassed the 30 percent target of the NEP by using a different methodology than the one used by the EPU. Thus, for the Ninth Malaysia Plan, the author argued for a more multi-racial approach to improve the country's competitiveness.

A few months after the submission of the report, the findings, particularly on the Malay equity attracted a lot of controversy. While I believe Dr Lim's methodology is debatable, the extent to which the whole episode descended spoke volumes about the siege mentality of the Malay community that has been fostered by the authorities all this while.

They argued that Dr Lim had a hidden agenda and that Malay equity was far below the 30 percent goal; they claimed, as calculated by the EPU under the Ninth Malaysia Plan, the figure was only 18.9 percent. The whole controversy would seem rather comical if it did not turn so ugly and racial: on the one hand, some Malays were defending the NEP by arguing that it had *failed* to achieve its objective, while a non-Malay academician with an allegedly 'chauvinistic' agenda was supposedly attacking the Policy by claiming that it had been *successful*. Furthermore, the Malays were the UMNO leaders who saw the NEP as the community's sacred cow.

Among other things, Dr Lim referred to the dominance of GLCs in the economy to support his case. As the GLCs are owned by the government, most of them are ostensibly tasked to push for greater Malay and Bumiputera participation in the economy in one way or another. This takes many forms: such as hiring Malay professionals, using Malay firms in their supply or production chains and providing scholarships to Malay students.

Outside the GLCs however, Malay participation in business, especially in multinational corporations and the SMEs, is still far from satisfactory. The SMEs are predominantly owned by the Chinese community.

The economic marginalisation of the Malays compounded with colonial propaganda led to Syed Hussein al-Attas' tour-de-force, *The Myth of the Lazy Native*. The argument was that the 'natives'—in this case the Malays—were naturally lazy and hence, justified the civilising mission of the West while simultaneously permitting the non-Malays to continue closing the door to commercial sectors on the Malays.

The separation of the Malays from colonial capitalism allowed the colonialists to define them as 'lazy natives'. Ironically, however, perpetuating race-based affirmative action that coddles the Malays only serves to reinforce the colonial stereotype as it creates a false sense of security among the Malays that lower standards can be relied on to succeed.

Today, globalisation constrains the governments around the world in new ways, the 2008 global financial crisis notwithstanding. This does not mean that governments do not have a role to play in the economy, but that they should be more strategic in order to benefit from the globalised environment. Hence, competition must be opened up so that the Malay middle class develops its skills to enable it to compete not only locally but internationally.

Tun Dr Mahathir Mohamad's privatisation exercise rested on the creation of GLCs and privatised projects. Yet, unlike British Prime Minister Margaret Thatcher, Mahathir merely shifted the bureaucrats from the government to the GLCs. In Britain, the privatised utilities were given the freedom to operate subject to a clear regulatory framework, but in Malaysia the framework was absent and many management decisions were referred to the government leadership.

This ersatz form of capitalism lies at the heart of many of Malaysia's economic problems and contributes directly to the Malay lag in business. And that is why many Malay businesses fail to make headway or even go under. They are tied to the government's (and indirectly, UMNO's) support and patronage networks, with all the inefficiency they bring. What is the result? A successful or bright young Malay entrepreneur comes onto the public stage and people immediately speculate who his political 'boss' is. This is, of course, horribly unfair and reflects the Catch-22 situation that many Malays who want to go into business find themselves in. The key to increasing Malay equity in my mind, therefore, is not to increase government activism in the economy, but to recalibrate it.

As elaborated above, there exist real and genuine problems in building Malay entrepreneurs. Much has been done since the implementation of the NEP to address these issues, but I believe that in order to empower genuine Malay entrepreneurs, we need to re-strategise vis-à-vis the GLCs.

First, anti-discriminatory policies must be introduced to prevent discrimination in the workforce. Malays frequently face discrimination in small- and medium-sized industries. It would be good if the non-Malays that dominate this sector actively get more Malays involved. But such a policy would require the opening up of other sectors of employment where the government and GLCs have enforced a policy of Malay-only preference.

Thus, both sides need to be ready for this to be introduced, but I believe that it is in the long-term interest of the Malays to get more Malays out of the comfort zone of government employment into the commercial sector, thus making Malay progress more independent and hence, more sustainable. This dynamism and competitiveness is essential to succeed in the globalised world.

More must also be done to increase non-Malay participation in the public sector. This will not only decrease the ethnic identification of economic activity, but will also go a long way in increasing our civil service's efficiency and delivery. A lot of the cultural misunderstandings that bedevil the relationship between the state and non-Malay citizens in the country today could have been avoided if our government departments were simply a bit more diverse.

All of this points to the crying need for our GLCs, and indeed all businesses in Malaysia, to stop acting like government bodies or hoping for the help of the public sector and embrace competition as well as the entrepreneurial spirit. Our economy has relied for far too long on the power of the state, and this has been the cause of it being held back. The Malaysian private sector, especially its Malay component must play its part in generating national prosperity, and the first step towards this is stepping away from the current economic regime. Should they do this, the government, in turn, must be supportive of this paradigm shift.

Beyond the GLCs, we need to cut the costs of doing business by removing red tape and making it easy for any budding entrepreneur to start his or her own business. This, combined with policies that support entrepreneurship as well as community trust organisations as outlined in the previous chapter will benefit Malays who lack capital and experience. By allowing businesses to flourish, they can contribute more to the economy.

There must also be stronger mechanisms to reduce political patronage and corruption in the business world as this kills incentive. The perception that to do business in Malaysia requires 'know-who' rather than 'know-how' reflects the seriousness of the problem. We need to empower the Malays with the talent, passion and enthusiasm to do business to prosper, not those with the right political connections.

Just as we provide the space for businesses to flourish, businesses must also be allowed to fail. Only under such an environment can we get a truly courageous and creative entrepreneurial spirit. No longer can we salvage businesses merely for their political connections.

A PEOPLE'S ECONOMY: THE SELANGOR EXPERIENCE

In His Royal Highness the Sultan of Selangor's Royal Address to the State Assembly in 2008, the term '*merakyatkan ekonomi Selangor*' (literally 'creating a people's economy') was first introduced to describe the different welfare measures introduced by the new Pakatan Rakyat state government.

Some of the measures were announced in the Keadilan and PAS joint-Selangor manifesto going into the 12th General Elections. This included a RM1,000 gift for those going to university, a RM100 trust fund for newborns (when implemented it was added that the money would be invested and could be withdrawn when they turn 18 to the amount of RM1,500), an old-age *takaful* scheme, 20 m^3 free water for individual residential consumers and a 90-day maternity leave for state civil servants, among others initiatives. But there were also other measures that were only announced by the PR state government after coming to power, among them a fund for estate workers and their families and a RM12 million grant for Chinese and Tamil-type national schools as well as independent religious schools.

The rationale behind these policies is that as Selangor is the richest and most developed state in Malaysia, it is only appropriate that the state government implements policies for the benefit of all its residents. Admittedly, these policies might seem rather limited in nature, but this is a paradigm shift where the public gets a share of the state's wealth. At the same time, wealth creation goes on. Any redistribution or welfare programme would be impossible without wealth being created. Investments in Selangor reached RM11 billion in 2008, the highest amount in over nine years.

Much of the funding for the People's Economy policies comes from better economic management. The state stopped many new joint-venture initiatives to develop state land with private parties that previously largely benefited the latter, who inevitably tended to be politically-connected companies. Instead, under the new administration, the state's own GLCs were either tasked to implement these projects themselves or to sell these projects entirely to private parties.

Some of the joint-venture partners were supposedly Bumiputera companies but most were actually Ali-Baba partners, trading their connections and names to get the deal only to farm it out to non-Bumiputera parties to do the actual work. This resulted in little, if any, capacity building for the Bumiputeras while the state lost out in terms of revenue.

For so long, that was the tragedy of Selangor—a rich state that was Malaysia's economic hub, its focus on quick profits was at the expense of the ordinary citizens. Many planning and regulatory provisions were ignored in order to help the developers. Squatters, who are predominantly Malays, were victimised by the previous administration's 'Zero Squatter' policy where the government proceeded to clear lucrative pieces of land for the sake of 'development' without due consideration to the residents, some of whom had been living there for decades.

In Seri Setia, my constituency, the BN state government sought to solve the problems of squatters in the Old Klang Road area. The residents of Taman Desaria attended a hearing in August 2003 that was held as required by law at the MBPJ to voice their objections. Among their objections was that the Mayor should not have chaired the meeting as one of the councillors had interest in the firm developing the project.

However, the residents did not realise that in March that year, the project was already given the go ahead. Only later, when the residents initiated a court action to compel MBPJ to issue a stop-work order, did they find this out. The judge later commented how the hearing was merely eyewash and a formality.

In a more sinister twist, the minutes of a state government committee were presented at the trial, purporting that the project was exempted from going through the normal planning process. When the residents examined the documents, it was discovered that two separate documents were presented at trial. The residents made a police report, contending that this amounted to forgery, but to this day, no action has been taken.

Today, the residents have to live side-by-side with Desa Mentari, the project that arose from these moves. It does not conform to density and planning requirements, oppressing both Desa Mentari's own residents as well as their neighbours in Taman Desaria.

Another example of the derelictions of the previous state government is Kampung Berembang, Ampang, situated within the shadows of the Petronas Twin Towers. A settlement of more than 30 years, the land it was built on became a gold mine as both Selangor and Kuala Lumpur developed. Ironically, the residents there were largely UMNO supporters.

In November 2006, as part of a joint-venture project involving a Selangor state subsidiary and a private party, Kampung Berembang was demolished, making nearly 500 residents homeless. Some of them were students, preparing for SPM and STPM examinations. Fires mysteriously broke out at two homes.

While no one questions the right of the developer to take over the land, the question is why this was done before alternative housing was completed? Why were such measures used?

In February 2009, under the PR state administration, the issue was resolved and the 68 affected families were given keys to their own homes. Now, the focus is to adhere to the existing guidelines and laws, and if those are inadequate, to introduce new policies. More often than not, the existing regulatory framework is adequate, but implementation has been poor. Our priority is to ensure that the people of Selangor never have to experience the kind of incredible abuses of state power that were wrought upon them over the last couple of decades.

A major hurdle that Selangor, like the rest of Malaysia faces is that the institutions have ceased to be independent due to political interference over that period of time. The recommendations and opinions of civil servants were frequently overridden by politicians, making many departments dysfunctional. The press and Opposition parties that could have played an active check-and-balance role were emasculated.

The long domination of BN in the country's politics has led to civil servants being unable to distinguish between the political party and the government. Some try to discharge their responsibilities conscientiously, but others are content to just follow orders. When added with the commercial pressures in Selangor that provide lucrative ways for those in authority to make quick money under the counter, it becomes a dangerous combination.

That is why after PR took over, we spent time building the trust of the civil servants. Added to the burden of solving a mess that is half a century old, it has not been easy to balance this with the expectations of the people who voted us in. An added complication is that some in our parties expected to benefit in the same way as BN members traditionally did.

Apart from these complications, there was also our complex and increasingly acrimonious relationship with the Federal government. Malaysia was born as a Federation with a division of powers between the Federal government and the state governments. However, due to the BN's overwhelming majority and long term in power, the spirit of Federalism has deteriorated.

Since the 12th General Elections, there have been several skirmishes with regards to Federal and state government relations in the PR states. The one major incident that stood out was regarding the water takeover by the state government from water concessionaires, which began during BN's leadership of the state government. When PR took over, we pushed through a deal that we thought was important to protect the interests of the state, while providing adequate compensation to the concessionaires. But the Federal government thwarted our offer, claiming that it was not sufficient.

In addition, we also discovered in 2009 documents of a meeting to set up a RM50 million 'People-Centric Programme' initiated by the Prime Minister's Department. In the documents, it was clearly stated that the objective of the programme was to strengthen support for the BN and weaken PR. What's more, in addition to other Federal departments being part of the meeting, the Election Commission was also included![10]

Our own political fortunes mean little, but what really rankled about this 'People-Centric Programme' was the fact that the Federal government was prepared to plunge the state into turmoil and make the people suffer simply to advance one side of the political fence. This sort of zero-sum behaviour is what poisons our politics today.

In spite of all the challenges, I believe we have exemplified the different ideals and philosophy of the new Selangor state government. True, more needs to be done, but we have to start somewhere.

---

10 <http://themalaysianinsider.com/index.php/malaysia/20276-pakatan-alleges-subversive-bn-plot-to-topple-selangor-government>

With a diverse population that is a microcosm of Malaysia and a rapidly developing economy, Selangor can be a showcase of how Malays can benefit through different policies that are not particularly race-based but more focused on merit and need as well as the sustenance of durable institutions that serve the people.

THE EDUCATION QUESTION

A DYNAMIC AND EQUITABLE EDUCATION POLICY

Education has also become another heated topic in our public discourse today. It grieves me, and one imagines, all sensible Malaysians that something so basic and noble should become an object of acrimonious and often savage dispute. As each side tries to weigh in by attempting to be louder or more extreme than the other, the voices of the students who suffer under the manifold idiocies of our current educational establishment go unheard. How do they suffer, you ask?

Malaysian university students who are fortunate to receive public scholarships, regardless of whether they pursue tertiary education abroad or locally, are required to attend a short course organised by BTN, a bureau under the Prime Minister's Department. Originally set up with the objective of instilling patriotism and civic consciousness among the young during the early years of the NEP in response to the vocal student movement of the '70s, it has evolved to become a political brainwashing programme.

By the time I attended it in 2003, we were told, with complete and earnest seriousness, of how the country was in danger of attack by 'foreign powers' (a catch-all for the normal bogeymen of Singapore, America and Israel) and of the supposed 'perversion' of Islam by PAS. The facilitators would provide a long 'history' of Malay backwardness and argue how the only way the Malays can survive is by maintaining the status quo.

One of the modules compares the number of Malays in critical academic and technical disciplines pre- and post-NEP. This aims to emphasise how far the Malays have lagged behind and how the participants should be thankful for the NEP. At the same time, it highlights that in many fields the Malays still have not reached the targeted percentage, thus justifying the need to defend the NEP at all cost.

The fact that Malaysian university students are still subjected to such Cold War programmes highlights just how far our national education system has declined under the BN. The rot has gone deep into the core and even government action, however drastic may not be enough to reverse it. What Malaysians, especially Malay Malaysians need is a complete overhaul of their attitude towards the very concept of education before positive changes can be made in this area. But first, the reasons for this terrible dropping-off of standards.

When the NEP was introduced, education was one of the main planks of the new policy. Prior to the NEP, educational performance of the Malays—as both a factor and a result of Malay underdevelopment—was dismally low. This resulted in a vicious cycle of backwardness. The NEP, as well as the pervasiveness of the student movement, resulted in the introduction of the University and University Colleges Act in 1971 that greatly curtailed the autonomy of the universities. The Ministry of Education could now control curriculum development as well as appointments of academic staff. Quotas were introduced for students as well as faculty members in order 'to reflect the racial composition of the country'. The baseline was 55 percent for Bumiputera students with additional quotas for specific programmes.

Even then, as my father would tell me, it was difficult to get sufficient Bumiputera students. He played a role in introducing the matriculation programme to bypass the sixth form system in schools. At the same time, the provision of university scholarships both for local and overseas study was expanded, especially for Bumiputera students.

As a result of the quota system in local universities, a greater number of Malaysians, especially non-Malays, chose to study overseas. However, with the recession as well as the imposition of full overseas fees for Malaysian students by the United Kingdom and Australia in the 1980s, this became more difficult for many families. Local private colleges began to appear as a result, providing joint-programmes with overseas universities. Legislation to regulate private colleges and universities, however, only came about in 1996. These laws provide for minimum standards that private institutions have to satisfy.

A number of private colleges has made great strides towards advancing the quality of education in the country. But partly due to the availability of places in public universities and scholarships, as well as their lack of means, there are fewer Malays in private institutions. In effect, the existence of private universities complete the social stratification in the education system—different vernacular schools at primary level, different pre-university systems and ultimately, different tertiary institutions—all separating Malays from non-Malays. It also crowds out resources for public universities to improve their standards as many experienced academicians leave the public institutions for a better career in the private sector.

This ethnic identification with educational streams has naturally led to the growing ethnic polarisation in Malaysia. Some blame the problem on the very existence of different streams, i.e., they believe that Malaysia's racial problems occur simply because there are private colleges or vernacular schools. Such arguments deflect the BN-led government's decades-old failure to provide quality education to all Malaysians. The situation lies not by shutting down private colleges or vernacular schools, but rather by making our public education system competitive with them.

Most crucially, we need to make our national schools the first choice for education again, as it was in the first few decades after Independence. This will require larger investments into our schools, particularly in the rural areas, to ensure they are equipped with better facilities. More allowances need to be provided for the best teachers in order for them to even consider teaching in far-flung schools in rural areas (where the students are predominantly Malay). The government needs to monitor closely schools with underperforming students, including the school management and the teachers. While it is true that many of the teachers struggle to cope with the numerous challenges that are present in these schools, we still need to demand more from them in order to push these students to succeed. Otherwise, underperformance will continue to be the norm.

A support system for students who need to improve their performance can be instituted, especially in rural areas as well as urban ghettoes. Teaching assistants can be hired in greater numbers for underperforming schools. We must also note that many problems affecting underperforming students stem from their lack of family support. This requires more than just government action but also a more comprehensive effort involving the local community including mosques, neighbourhood and social organisations to ensure that parents give due attention to their children's education.

The principle of Early Intervention,[11] as articulated by the Centre for Social Justice in the United Kingdom, should also be vigorously adopted for such children to prevent them from dropping out or underachieving. A great recommendation that this strategy carries is that it was formulated by a bi-partisan team of both Labour and Conservative thinkers. If only such a spirit could exist here!

For secondary schools, greater consideration must be provided to implement a flexible system that can accommodate the best and brightest Malaysians. At present, all Malaysians generally have to go through the same system for the first fifteen years of their lives regardless

---

11 The Paper on Early Intervention can be found at: <http://www.centreforsocialjustice.org.uk/client/downloads/CSJ%20Early%20Intervention%20paper%20WEB%20(2).pdf>.

of ability. As a result, many gifted students become frustrated and are unable to realise their potential to the fullest. The brightest students should be identified early and nurtured to explore their potential.

This would mean that many Malays, who would otherwise be unable to go to private and international schools (not forgetting those who cannot afford to go to school overseas, particularly in Singapore), could experience a more competitive educational environment, and be fast-tracked in the education system. The system can be designed in such a way that those from the most deprived backgrounds are given more leeway to get into the best schools. This can thus increase their opportunities and raise their aspirations to succeed.

One possible way is by the creation of a Unified Stream, incorporating the different streams under one single-session school system with autonomy being thrown into the equation, in order to attract the schools to come together. Allow me to explain this concept, which is at this point merely a humble proposal that can and probably will be altered with the exigencies of time.

The Unified Stream is not, like certain quarters would wish, the unilateral absorption of all existing educational streams into the national system. Rather, it is something whereby the best features of the national stream (which has unfortunately, but understandably lost all credibility with many Malaysian parents, including Malay ones) are merged with the best of the vernacular schools into something altogether new and different.

In these Unified Stream schools, emphasis would be given to the national language, English as well as the added feature of vernacular education. This will mean that all students under this stream, regardless of their race, will be made to learn their mother tongue as well as another language, be it Mandarin or Tamil or one of the East Malaysian languages.

Such an arrangement, in effect, means a multi-lingual education for them. I can already hear the howls of the language nationalists, but consider the benefits of this. The children will primarily be taught in Malay for obvious reasons and they will also learn English, which is and will probably remain a global *lingua franca*. They will also be encouraged and, in fact, mandated to learn their mother tongue.

But they will also have the advantage of picking up another language, which is a huge advantage, especially if one of them is Mandarin or Tamil given the rise of China and India to economic prominence. In no way will this new system challenge the position of the national language. Rather, it highlights a multi-lingual and multi-cultural ethos, which can find no better expression than if our people can speak many languages well that is sadly not the case currently.

In addition, moral studies in Unified Stream schools can be scrapped in favour of general religious education for the non-Muslims, while all students would be required to pursue a subject about civil and cultural education that teaches them the historical, constitutional and cultural background of Malaysia. Vernacular schools, I should add, ought to be encouraged to incorporate such a subject into their curriculum if they are not doing something similar already, and those that do so must be given the proper incentives by the government.

The Unified Stream can provide a more in-depth teaching of Islam for Muslim students to inculcate in them broader and more holistic knowledge. To make this happen, single-session schooling will have to be put into practice, something that has been clamoured for countless of times in the past but which has not come to pass.

Now, I don't for one moment expect this Unified Stream to be an instant success or become an overnight panacea to our educational ills. Like all things in life, the devil will be in the detail and the actual implementation of the Unified Stream will require a careful but also bold reworking of our education establishment on all levels, be it funding or the training of our teachers.

Neither am I, by putting forward the Unified Stream, advocating that either national or vernacular schools be completely abolished in its favour. Schools should be allowed to join the Unified Stream voluntarily. In the case of the national schools, this will mean that the government and educational authorities will have to take a step back and leave the decision to the school's respective faculties and parents.

In any case, all schools, whether national or vernacular, that choose to remain outside the Unified Stream should still continue to be given whatever support they enjoyed from the government previously. The Unified Stream in effect is something completely voluntary, and even schools that decide to stand apart will benefit in that they would have been given some measure of autonomy. One would hope that the Unified Stream blossoms until more if not most other schools choose to join its banner, but with the proviso that those that do not will not be cast out or sidelined.

Many will scoff at such plans for greater autonomy, especially for national schools, but let us not forget that the blueprint for such a change already exists. Schools in the Unified Stream along with other selected schools such as fully-residential schools and premier schools can be given greater flexibility such as envisioned in the Cluster Schools introduced under the National Education Blueprint in 2007. Unfortunately, like other plans such as the Smart Schools in the past, little has come out of this idea, probably due to bureaucratic inertia.

Similarly, greater autonomy should be granted to our public universities where the majority of the students are Malays. Top universities such as the University of Malaya and Universiti Sains Malaysia can be liberalised so that a greater proportion of students can be chosen based on merit with allowance for need (while balancing it with the need to preserve diversity).

While the Apex University policy is a step in the right direction, more needs to be done. They can be provided with greater funds to attract top lecturers not only within Malaysia but from across the globe. This will ensure that they can compete with the likes of the National University of Singapore, which historically evolved from the

University of Malaya in Singapore. The same system of emphasising merit, need and diversity and placing less importance on race can be introduced across other universities to improve the standing of our institutions.

Currently, there exists a glass ceiling for non-Malays in teaching positions in public universities. Again, while I agree that there must be semblance of racial diversity, the major criterion should be merit. Indeed, the politicisation of academia in Malaysia has meant that even the best Malays are sidelined, in favour of those who are willing to become the political tools of the ruling regime.

Getting the best lecturers and academicians will benefit *all* students. The idea that only Malay academicians can take care of the welfare of Malay students must be challenged. Obviously, strict guidelines must be put in place to prevent discrimination against student of all races in universities, as universities should focus on promoting critical thinking and academic excellence.

At the same time, the government can regulate private institutions of higher learning more stringently and preserve the quality of education. Private institutions that do not meet minimum standards must be slapped with stiff penalties and even closed down, to ensure the quality of our education.

Another contentious issue is the scholarships provided by the PSD and GLCs which were also a prime factor in the creation of a Malay middle class. At present, the situation is in a mess with PSD scholars mostly being able to escape working for the government, while some are even working overseas, putting a lot of taxpayers' money to waste.

But there are GLCs that strictly enforce the requirement for the scholars to serve them but do not utilise them efficiently, resulting in a poor return on investment.

At the same time, the irony is that as the bulk of these scholarship recipients are Malays, many bright young Malays are trapped in jobs that do not push them to fulfil their potential, while the non-Malays reap the best jobs in the market. The latter, unfortunately, tend to come from the richer segments of those ethnic groups, and so social mobility is also increasingly coming to a standstill amongst the Chinese and Indians.

Returning to the issue of bonds, it is true that the contractual obligation to their sponsors lasts only about five to ten years, but as these are the formative years of their careers, they have a significant impact on the development of Malay professionals. However, we must not disregard the fact that there is no point for the PSD and GLCs to invest in sending students to the best universities abroad if they cannot get the scholars to work for them.

One way is to provide a flexible period for graduates to serve their contract of service. The PSD scholarship system should be integrated with the Diplomatic and Administrative Officers service as well as the GLCs. Bonds can still be for five- to ten-year stretches, but they should be allowed to choose to finish their contract terms anytime within, say, 15 to 20 years.

Admittedly, there is a chance that some might land a well-paying job allowing them or their employers to buy out the contract. This is a real risk, but the government and GLCs should consider this as part of their contribution to national interest, especially since their financial outlay is being reimbursed.

Furthermore, many GLCs have diverse subsidiaries and associated companies, and they should allow their scholars to gain different experiences and perspectives through working in these different companies. This exposes these graduates to the best practices locally and internationally in order for them to develop professionally and contribute to their respective sponsors.

Ultimately, in order for Malays to move forward in education, we must challenge the attitude that the Malays will always be left behind under a system that promotes meritocracy. It speaks volumes about the state of the Malays when meritocracy is seen as a threat.

In a globalised world, a competitive environment is crucial in order for the Malays to improve. We must not sacrifice educational standards in order to ensure Malay quotas are filled; it would be more meaningful if other methods such as intensive classes are used to help academically poor Malay students especially from deprived backgrounds while leaving minimum educational standards as they are. Otherwise, it is the Malays who will suffer most of all.

Attracting the best non-Malays to return home will eventually benefit other Malays as well. Malay underperformance in education can be divided into two broad factors: socio-economic factors and culture. Allowing Malays from poorer backgrounds special access to education is important in getting them to improve their socio-economic status, but getting capable Malays to compete on a level playing field is crucial to change their culture from one of dependence to one based on self-reliance. This latter development would be reinforced when achievements are regarded as attained on a level rather than an uneven playing field, thus forming a virtuous rather than a vicious cycle.

OTHER MEN'S TONGUES: THE VERNACULAR ISSUE

The medium of education remains a divisive issue in Malaysian politics. There are those who view vernacular schools with suspicion, taking it as evidence that the non-Malays are not serious about national integration and learning the national language. On the other hand, there are those who are increasingly dissatisfied with the quality as well as the inclusivity of the national schools.

Both sides have valid concerns. The national school system is in deep doldrums and as mentioned earlier, has been totally written off by many Malaysians. We must also recognise the invaluable contribution vernacular schools have made to Malaysia's progress. There are, after all, increasingly many Malays who accept this argument to the point that in 1999, it was estimated that 60,000 Malay students attended Chinese schools. As I have also stressed earlier, the issues of ethnic polarisation will not disappear overnight if these vernacular schools are done away with and one imagines that such a move will, in fact, deepen the divisions in our society.

In order to move forward, several changes need to be introduced to our education system to ensure that we keep up with the ever-changing times. Of the many aspects covered in this book, education is crucial to get the Malays to progress and catch up with the other communities, just as an emphasis on education propelled backwater Asian countries such as Korea, Taiwan and Singapore to progress rapidly in the second half of the 20th century to become developed nations.

Greater space must be given to mother-tongue education in national schools while accommodating the diverse nature of Malaysian society, but to achieve national unity, we must also be daring enough to recognise the challenges the existence of vernacular and private schools pose to us.

It's a painful thing to say, but many Malays view the national-type schools with suspicion, even as sinister entities because they know very little about them, and this is a gap in knowledge that the vernacular education movement has done little to counter. Ask an average Malay, or even a Chinese or Indian who was educated in another stream about what goes on in national-type schools and you are likely to draw a blank or the basic stereotypes.

If some sectors view Chinese schools and Indian schools as divisive to national unity, it could be because the educationists that animate these schools have not done a better job communicating with their counterparts from other ethnic groups. It is a sad sight to see the instructors of youth, all of whom have undertaken the sacred duty to train and educate the young, bickering with each other when really, all of them want the same thing.

This is not an indictment of either Malay, Chinese or Indian educationists, but rather a demonstration of the pitiful state of affairs that years of BN mismanagement has left our country in. One really hopes that the educationists of Malaysia, regardless of their ethnicity, will someday be able to set aside their sectarian differences to push for better standards, the empowerment of parents as well as teachers and to end the abuse of governmental power in the field of education.

Vernacular schools need not only protect the cultural and linguistic values of the other races, but also contribute towards nation-building. Their schools should allocate more time towards civic and cultural consciousness and understanding Malaysia's diverse nature.

What do their teachers tell the students about other ethnic groups? How are the various ethnic groups portrayed in textbooks or school exercises? Is any mention or provision to educate the students about other cultures made, especially minority cultures such as the indigenous peoples of Sabah and Sarawak? Please note that I am not accusing the vernacular schools of not having or wanting to offer such facilities.

What I am saying, however, is that a lot of the criticisms and suspicions against them could be blunted or dispelled if it could be proven that they were producing Malaysians who could communicate with their follow citizens, who are capable of functioning and are comfortable existing in a multi-racial society.

I have not the slightest doubt in my mind that this is the goal of most vernacular school teachers and administrators. They need our support, and they also need to uncompromisingly combat their colleagues who are against the goal of greater national integration.

At the same time, it makes no sense for Malays to chastise the non-Malays for not having faith in national schools when little is said about the quality and inclusiveness of these schools, just as it makes no sense for the non-Malays to not realise that vernacular schools must play a greater role in fostering a true Bangsa Malaysia identity.

Again and again, it all boils down to a lack of communication. Could all of our problems be due to the fact that we do not know enough about each other and how we live our lives? We are so close but yet so separate.

This brings us to the question of exclusive Bumiputera institutions. The general thrust of this book has been for greater openness and less reliance on race-based quotas. However, I believe that the Malays might be more open to the idea of opening up Universiti Teknologi MARA or even my alma mater MCKK if the non-Malays are willing to give up the vernacular schools. This, of course, is another complicated issue in itself, and I would not dwell too much on this matter as my focus is on the broader education system.

Having said that, I must note how alarming it is that Malays are more concerned about exclusive student populations than the standards of education. In 2008, shortly before the Permatang Pauh by-election, Tan Sri Dato' Abdul Khalid Ibrahim was asked by a journalist to comment on the suggestion that Universiti Teknologi MARA open 10 percent of its student intake to non-Malays. Khalid's comments were quite neutral, namely that the suggestion must be studied thoroughly as the university was founded with the mission of uplifting Malay students by the creation of Malay professionals, but if the proposal was found to be effective in making Malays more competitive and motivated, then it should be considered.

The Malay press, predictably, broke out in a frenzy, while the usually docile students gathered by the hundreds to protest. Yet, when Malaysian universities dropped further down in international rankings, there was no outcry. Would it not make more sense to take in a proportion of non-Malay students if it leads to an improvement in our educational standards?

Some might question the relevance of diversity as a criterion for determining student intake. Although I believe that it should rank after merit and need, I still think there is significant value in using it as a criterion for university intake (and by extension, for the awarding of scholarships and government employment). I believe that learning to live in a diverse environment is a crucial part of education, especially in a plural society like Malaysia.

Even in the US, there is objection to the affirmative action for African-Americans who normally lag behind the other communities (Asian-Americans who perform above average often argue that they are penalised in university admissions), it is broadly accepted that relying on merit alone would mean that Asian Americans would disproportionately dominate universities. Universities there define this 'enrolment goal' to provide 'ethnic diversity'. Admittedly, however, there is a danger that it can lead to a slippery slope—which is why I stated that diversity should only come into the picture after taking into account merit and need.

Education in Malaysia has become extremely polarised and is a major issue in our cultural wars. This has to stop. A good education system is in the interest of every Malaysian parent. Only when we accept that basic premise can we start looking at a new paradigm in our education system.

Compromise and goodwill is the key—this is something that is needed on both sides of the education question; it is not a question of who needs to 'take the first step'. We all care for the future of our children and that, rather than our sectarian rivalries, should be our guiding principle.

THE MENTARI PROJECT

When the debate on the teaching of Science and Mathematics in English intensified in early 2009, I felt it important for those who supported the policy to understand the crux of the issue. As I turned over the various arguments for and against the policy, my mind kept turning back to two community service initiatives that I had the privilege of being involved in, namely Projek Kalsom and the Mentari Project.

The plight of Kelthom Abdullah, a single mother from Kelantan was highlighted by a Malaysian newspaper in 1993. She did not have enough to make ends meet and her children dropped out of school. This caught the attention of a group of Malaysian students studying in Britain, and they decided to raise some money to help her and her children. But the students thought that more needed to be done and went a step further. They started a motivational programme for secondary school students in rural Malaysia. Every year, during the summer holidays, Malaysian tertiary students from overseas and local institutions would go to a rural area to motivate the secondary school students, which the former called Projek Kalsom.

I had heard so much about the project and was fortunate to have taken part as a facilitator in 2004, when it was held in SM Tengku Mahmud Besut, Terengganu. It was difficult to get the students to participate in any activity in English. They would just put on a poker face and keep quiet. Our education system had shaped their outlook and they felt that it was only worth participating in if you could answer correctly. But a few girls dared to take part in spite of their broken English. One of them even spoke with a British accent as she was an avid fan of Harry Potter! Another managed to give a full speech in English at the end of the programme.

Initiatives like Projek Kalsom are a rebuke to the calumny that the youth of Malaysia are apathetic or not socially-conscious. The youth deserve our full support. This project not only benefits the targeted groups but also the volunteers themselves. In my case, it helped in my work for what eventually became the Mentari Project.

In January 2008, a few friends and I, including a former teacher, decided to start a voluntary tuition project among primary school students in Desa Mentari, which is where the Project took its name from. As I mentioned earlier, part of the inspiration for the Mentari initiative came from Projek Kalsom. I also felt that this was an important service that had to be provided in my urban Kelana Jaya area.

One thing I found very striking during the pilot class, was that when I asked the students what their favourite subject was, not one of them answered Science. When I probed them as to why this was the case, a girl replied, "It's difficult as we cannot understand English." The others nodded in agreement. Most of the parents who sent their kids to the programme were concerned about their children's education, but they could not even assist them in the most basic exercises due to the language barrier.

My experiences in community service revealed to me yet another of the many problems facing Malaysian education. While our leaders bicker over grand plans and petty details, the students themselves, Malays included, suffer due to hastily-conceived and top-down measures.

Indeed, one such disastrous policy has been the introduction of the teaching of Science and Mathematics in English by Tun Dr Mahathir

Mohamad in 2003. Supposedly concerned with the deteriorating command of English among the younger generation, the then PM decided to dismantle a policy long fought for by many Malay intellectuals, ostensibly with the intention of improving the standard of English. It was pushed through without proper consultation with parents, teachers or Malay intellectuals. When people voiced their concerns about the ability of teachers, who had been schooled under the Malay medium for so long, teaching in English, the authorities argued that this could be overcome by using multimedia aids! On the other hand, due to vocal opposition from the Chinese educationists, the government allowed Chinese schools to teach the two subjects in both English and Mandarin.

Unsurprisingly, the policy ran into trouble almost immediately. Students from poorer families and rural backgrounds, especially the Malays, struggle to cope with the new system. One also imagines that this is the case for their urban-poor counterparts, including Chinese and Indians who come from non-English speaking homes, or the children of Sabah and Sarawak from similar backgrounds.

Even more distressing is the reality that many teachers were also unable to help as they themselves are not proficient in English. Yet, the system requires them to teach in English while the students are still given the option to answer either in Malay or English. But the concession for choice of language in the exam does not amount to much as most cannot follow the subject from the outset as the teaching is done in English.

Not only does this not help much in improving the level of English proficiency, but it also creates a bigger gap between the middle class, and the rural and working class. This has led many Malaysians to oppose this policy, not so much because of their ideology or ethnic background but simply because it has failed to work.

Thus, I support the decision by the Federal government in 2009 to dismantle the policy, having realised, what we had insisted from the beginning, that the policy did not work.

In terms of the teaching of English, the subject needs to be intensified and implemented in a creative manner to promote student understanding of the language from an early age. Teaching can be expanded at secondary and tertiary levels, as no one can dispute the importance of English in today's world, especially in allowing Malay students to compete with other Malaysians and people from across the world.

I must stress here that I accept the mastery of English is crucial at more advanced and specialised levels of education. That is why while I support the dismantling of the policy, I do not share some of the more xenophobic and extreme arguments against English advanced by some who are against the policy.

Rather, one feels that quality should override quantity if the standard of English, and indeed Science and Mathematics, in our schools is to be improved. The policy that has damaged these subjects has gone on for too long and has not shown enough results to justify its continuation. It is far too muddled and for the good of the three academic disciplines, it has to be replaced with something more flexible.

Also, as touched upon in the previous section, there are also other issues that we need to contend with and which are often ignored in our debate on education. As I have stressed countless times, we not only need a change in governmental policies but also a shift in how we think about education in the first place.

None of this is new to anyone in the know. There's too much emphasis on passing exams and getting paper qualifications. It is easy to blame this all on the government (and it is probably its fault, mostly), but parents must also take charge of their children's education. Malaysians need to get involved and realise that educational institutions are not degree silos, but places for the development and training of all-rounded people and citizens.

In the Mentari Project, we sought to go beyond the Malaysian obsession with exam results and focus on learning skills as well, as we felt that would be more effective for the Desa Mentari children in the long run. Hence, the classes involved a lot of games to make learning fun. The children loved it and soon became more assertive and confident, a different lot from the ones who initially joined the project.

But the parents were not too amused when the tales of the fun and play reached them. They thought more needed to be done on drilling the students to get good results in exams. Eventually, we gave more room to focus on exams, particularly for the Year Six students who would be sitting their UPSR examinations, but we continued to slot in some educational games to develop their learning skills.

I am aware that much of our teaching may be unconventional but the difference, however small, that we make in the children of Desa Mentari's lives overrides such concerns. It is my earnest wish that projects like Mentari and Kalsom can continue to grow so that all Malaysian children in need can one day benefit from them.

ISLAM IN A MULTICULTURAL SOCIETY

CELEBRATING OUR TRADITION OF MODERATION

On 7 July 2005, I hopped on the London Underground as was my habit. It was my last day at work as a part-time telephone interviewer and I was eager to get the day out of the way, but the system suddenly broke down. Initially, I thought that it was just another case of London's ancient infrastructure falling apart. I guess the problem of poor public transport isn't unique to Malaysia!

Later, I found out that several bombings had occurred across the city—the closest being less than a kilometre away from the station I was at. Three bombs exploded in the Underground, while a fourth blew up a double-decker bus, killing 52 commuters along with the four suicide bombers. This, as we know, was the terrible London Bombings of 2005, four years after the 11 September terrorist attacks on America.

It transpired that four Muslims had carried out the bombings, purportedly out of anger at British support for the US-led invasion of Iraq. Like many Muslims, no matter how angry we had been at the misguided foreign policies of the West, I was saddened by the incident. After all, I was so close to where it took place. I shudder to think what could have happened had I, a fellow Muslim brother who had protested against the invasion, been closer to the scene of the attacks. It led me to wonder what had happened to some Muslims that led them to forget our tradition of moderation.

When I was 14 years old, I read *The Autobiography of Malcolm X*. I remember that one of the most compelling parts of the book was when he described his pilgrimage to Mecca, having rejected the racial-based tenets of the Black Muslim Nation of Islam:

> During the past eleven days here in the Muslim world, I have eaten from the same plate, drunk from the same glass, and slept in the same bed (or on the same rug)—while praying to the same God—with fellow Muslims, whose eyes were the bluest of blue, whose hair was the blondest of blond, and whose skin was the whitest of white. And in the words and in the actions in the deeds of the 'white' Muslims, I felt the same sincerity that I felt among the black African Muslims of Nigeria, Sudan, and Ghana.
>
> We were truly all the same (brothers)—because their belief in one God had removed the white from their minds, the white from their behaviour, and the white from their attitude.
>
> I could see from this, that perhaps if white Americans could accept the Oneness of God, then perhaps, too, they could accept in reality the Oneness of Man—and cease to measure, and hinder, and harm others in terms of their 'differences' in colour.

What was significant was that the pilgrimage to Mecca had effected a change of heart in Malcolm X. Here was a man who had been a staunch advocate of African-American ethno-nationalism and reverse racism, who now recognised the need to rise above race after embracing the true form of the Muslim faith. Truly, this signified the centrality of the universal brotherhood of man to the teachings of Islam.

In Malaysia, however, Islam has almost become inexorably linked to the Malay race and the two are often spoken and thought of as interchangeable. This has regrettably brought the Islamic faith into the equation of our national ethnic conflicts and rivalries, much to its detriment. At the same time, the Muslims of Malaysia have been beset by the same socio-political and economic problems of the Muslim *ummah* on a global scale. What is the cause of all this and what is the way out?

We must first understand the roots of our faith, in particular, to the time when Islam first came to the region. The spread of Islam to Southeast Asia allowed for the flowering of a unique heritage. Largely spread by traders, Sufi sheikhs and feudal rulers who had converted, the Islam that grew in Southeast Asia is, by and large, rooted in the moderate tradition. The cultural aspects of the local population were incorporated into the Muslim legacy, and the community had no problems in transforming themselves into a plural society. The tradition of moderation in the Malay world has rested largely on the three pillars of Shafie' *fiqh*, Asha'ari theology and Ghazalian Sufism. As Datuk Seri Anwar Ibrahim wrote in *The Asian Renaissance*:

> This peaceful and gradual Islamisation has moulded the Southeast Asian Muslim psyche into one which is cosmopolitan, open-minded, tolerant and amenable to cultural diversity.

Not long after I started working for Anwar, I was part of his entourage that was invited to visit a *pesantren* (an Indonesian traditional *madrasa*) about two hours by road from Surabaya, deep inside the Javanese heartland. It was constructed near the tomb of one of the nine saints of Java, the Wali Songo.

"The saints spread Islam by incorporating the culture of the

Javanese, not by opposing it. They adopted shadow puppets, the *gamelan* orchestra and the *silat* art of self-defence in spreading Islam," said one of the *kiyai*s or imams of the *pesantren*. "This peaceful approach created the largest Muslim community in the world. Doesn't that tell us something?"

Indeed, the spread of Islam in the Malay world has exemplified this tradition of moderation. As Muslims gradually learned to adopt different responses to modernity and the West, some resisted interactions altogether, seeing the West as representing a Godless and alien civilisation. Others, especially the elite, chose to adopt Western ideology wholesale, believing that European civilisation represented the future and only by imitating the Europeans could Muslims achieve a revival. But the majority sought to distil the different components of Western influence and to pick and choose the elements which were compatible with Islam for Muslims to progress.

Through the years, the broad trends remain the same, although they have manifested themselves in different ways. The first group, the literalists, argues that the West is diametrically opposed to the faith and must be rejected *in toto*. They do not regard the adoption of Western technology as problematic, but what they resist is Western thought. In their opinion, modern Western thinking is shaped by a secular experience that is completely alien to Islam and therefore, must be rejected in its entirety. They contend that Islam must be interpreted literally in our daily lives. The literalists prefer a quick fix, focused on superficialities, to cure the ills of the modern and materialistic world.

A small and extreme fringe from this group advocates the use of violence to advance their cause, even against civilians. They tap into the anger at the injustices experienced by Muslims across the world but choose to ignore the principles established by our religion— with the 11 September 2001 terrorist attacks on the US as the most potent example. No matter how misguided the policy of the Western governments, killing innocent civilians cannot be condoned at any time. As a result, we lose the moral high ground that should be the natural position of all Muslims.

Following a revival of Islam as well as the advancement of information and communication technology, Muslims have become very concerned about problems affecting their brethren across the world. Malays are now more exposed to the problems in Palestine, Chechnya and Iraq. There is nothing wrong in that, as Islam enjoins its adherents to be concerned about the plight affecting the Muslim *ummah*. What becomes problematic is when we ignore problems affecting our fellow citizens at home in our excitement over global concerns.

As Malaysian jurist, Sheikh Dr Mohammad Afifi al-Akiti, wrote in his *fatwa* against suicide bombing:

> We should have been taught from childhood by our fathers and mothers about the need to prioritise and about how to reconcile the spheres of our global concerns with those of our local responsibilities—as we will definitely not escape the questioning in the grave about the latter— so that by this insight we may hope that our response will not be disproportionate nor inappropriate.

The second group, a group I label 'the liberal fundamentalists' contends that the problem lies strictly within Islam. They advocate expanding the power of *ijtihad* to all Muslims to free us from the shackles of the rigid thinking of our scholars in the past. This, they feel, would solve all our problems. They argue that Islam in its entirety must be made to correspond to modern liberal ideals. Furthermore, they believe that the Muslim world must adopt Western values in its entirety. In effect, they seek a European-style Reformation of the faith, intending to reform Islam from outside the framework of the religion.

Muslims must strive to regain our position as the moderate and exemplary *ummah—ummatan wasattan*—where we strive to make a difference among Muslims and non-Muslims alike. After all, the Prophet Muhammad (peace be upon him) was sent as *rahmatan lil alamin*: a blessing to all mankind; not just Muslims.

I was first introduced to Tariq Ramadan, a Swiss-born Muslim intellectual at events organised by the Federation of Students Islamic Societies (FOSIS) in the UK. He also happens to be the grandson of As-Shahid Imam Hassan al Banna, the founder of the Muslim Brotherhood in Egypt and the son of Said Ramadan, the ideologue of the Brotherhood. Ramadan has contributed immensely to the debate on how Western Muslims can be both faithful to Islam and simultaneously live in harmony in the Western context. In *Western Muslims and the Future of Islam*, he lamented on the schizophrenia of many Muslim communities in the West:

> The universal message of Islam that should move Muslims' civic conscience to promote justice, right and goodness everywhere is reduced to this: 'since we are a feeble minority'—a defensive, self-pitying discourse, narrowly concerned with the protection of self and 'the community' ...
>
> It is true that these rights sometimes have to be defended on behalf of a particular community that is facing discrimination, but ... that does not mean perverting one's civic action by reducing it to a mere defence of 'my religion', 'my culture', or 'my ethnic group'. The principles that undergird the 'community of faith' require that we act against communitarianism and the thinking of the ghetto and sectarianism...

The role of Muslim communities in the West is to defend principles, not interests, and if it transpires that it is in their interest to have their universal principles respected, it should be clear that their fight for these principles serve society as a whole ...

Replace 'minority' with 'majority' and the same observations and arguments can be made about the Malays in Malaysia. Another example is Singapore. Although the city-state is in Southeast Asia and has an indigenous Malay Muslim community, Muslims are a minority in its diverse society.

I met Dr Albakri Ahmad from the Islamic Religious Council in Singapore in 2008 and asked for his opinion on how the Muslim authorities cope with a stronger religious consciousness while being a minority community in a secular society. He emphasised that Muslims were taught that part and parcel of being a good Muslim is being a good citizen.

Before any government policy is implemented, a lot of discussion and consultation with the various stakeholders take place. Religious leaders in turn then explain their position to the government and an acceptable policy is negotiated. Changes are implemented at a manageable pace, avoiding as much public controversy as possible in favour of closed-door discussions and deliberations. Muslims should look back at our history and realise that we were strongest when we were most tolerant, because we observed a key element of our faith. We did not betray the teachings of Islam in this, but instead, we were actually being faithful to it. Let us not forget that the Medina Charter promulgated by the Prophet Muhammad guaranteed the rights of the non-Muslim people living in the city.

Whenever we are tempted to stifle the construction of a non-Muslim place of worship, we should reflect upon how Caliph Umar al-Khattab declined the invitation of Sophronius, the Patriarch of Jerusalem to pray in the Church of Holy Sepulchre after conquering the city. Umar refused because he feared that his action would lead to Muslims in the future taking away the place of worship from Christians.

Both Muslim Andalucía and Ottoman Turkey treated their non-Muslim inhabitants—especially Christians and Jews—well. The 'People of the Book', as they were known, participated as traders, translators and even viziers in the Muslim court. In fact, a Jew, Samuel ibn Nagrela al Nagid, led Granada's Muslim army in the 11th century! In the following century, Musa ibn Maimun (known to the West as Maimonides), medieval Judaism's most celebrated scholar, left Andalucía following persecution by some Muslim groups there, but chose to migrate to Morocco, Palestine and eventually Egypt — all Muslim lands. In Egypt, he became a physician to Salahuddin al-Ayubi, known to the West as Saladin.

Salahuddin was well-regarded for his exemplary chivalry, not just among Muslims but also in the West. Considering that he was the one who managed to recapture Jerusalem from the Christians, this was no mean feat indeed! Catholicism's most remarkable medieval poet, Dante Alighieri, wrote in his magnum opus *The Divine Comedy*, that he was placed in limbo, between heaven and hell, along with the heroes of Troy and Rome for his exemplary character: "I saw great Saladin, aloof, alone."

There is, in fact, an incredible example of his nobility in the movie *Kingdom of Heaven*. Contrary to previous Hollywood depictions of Muslims as sinister or villainous, Salahuddin is depicted as peace-loving and just. Towards the end of the movie, he enters a church having just re-conquered Jerusalem from the Crusaders. In there, he notices a crucifix on the ground, having been knocked down from the altar nearby. Carefully, he picks it up with both his hands and sets it on the table again before leaving, taking care not to step on the parts of the church's floor where the cross had been carved in. It has been reported that the cinema-goers in Lebanon cheered at this scene of *Kingdom of Heaven*.[12] While this incident was probably not historical, it is a good representation of the kind of man Salahuddin was. He is definitely a model for Muslim leaders to aspire to in this aspect.

Ottoman Turkey included major parts of Eastern Europe, North Africa and West Asia and the majority of its subjects were not Muslims. Following the fall of Muslim Andalucía and the Spanish Inquisition, both Muslims and Jews fled to the empire to escape persecution. Salonika, in Greece, became the largest Jewish city in Europe but included many Muslims and Christians. Ironically, this peaceful coexistence was shattered following the onslaught of nationalism: Firstly, in the early 20th century the Muslims were replaced by Turkish Christians although many of them were Greek; secondly, during the Second World War, the Jews either fled or were killed en masse. The Ottoman Empire too had its own issues resulting in the Armenian massacres during the First World War. Even then, stories abound of Muslim leaders who stood up and rescued many victims of the tragic event.

Unfortunately today, many Muslims are stuck in a siege mentality. We waste a lot of time being concerned about conspiracy theories— while real, immediate and tangible challenges that exist in our midst are ignored. Any criticism of Muslims is decried as part of a sinister Western agenda, without any examination of its merits.

At the same time, our tradition of tolerance and openness has been forgotten. We forget the importance of ethics or *adab* when we engage in polemics, as it denigrates into *takfir* or terming each other as infidels. We always shout about 'human rights' when we are the minority in the West, but do we accord the same treatment to the minority at home? The bottom line is, as Muslims seek to achieve justice, we must do so by being sincere to the principles taught by our religion, best expressed by the Quranic injunction:

---

12 http://www.lebanonwire.com/0605/05061201CP.asp

> O ye who believe! Stand out firmly for Allah, as witnesses to fair dealing, and let not the hatred of others to you make you swerve to wrong and depart from justice. Be just: that is next to piety: and fear Allah. For Allah is well-acquainted with all that ye do. (Al-Maidah 5:8)

I was in Britain when Tony Blair and George W. Bush decided to invade Iraq in 2003. I was fortunate to be part of several of the demonstrations of the Anti-War movement, including the largest in February 2003 on the eve of the war when approximately two million people descended upon central London to protest the War. The entire spectrum of British society was involved: trade unionists, socialists and peaceniks; Christians, Muslims and atheists. This allowed Muslims to be in the mainstream and work together with civil society in opposing that misguided decision.

Later, I was among the FOSIS delegates elected to represent my university at the National Union of Students Conference. Largely due to the efforts by a fellow Malaysian, Wan Mohd Firdaus Wan Fuaad, the Muslim student representation in the NUS increased significantly between 2004 and 2005. We learned that while we had our concerns—from immediate ones such as provision of prayer rooms and *halal* food, to broader ones such as combating Islamophobia and opposing the War on Iraq—others would only take our concerns seriously if we were willing to consider theirs.

By doing so, we eventually succeeded in securing many of our demands and at the same time portrayed a pragmatic and positive image for Muslim students in general. What do all these lessons teach us? How can our generation build on Islam's rich heritage to move forward in a diverse society both locally and globally?

Firstly, Malay Muslims need to focus on addressing our immediate challenges: both inter-ethnic and intra-ethnic socio-economic disparity, lack of access to education, discrimination against women.

Too often the youth are exposed to either the utopia of the literalists or the agnosticism of the liberals and focus on these abstract issues without seeing the bigger picture. As Muslims, we should not only be able to confidently address the issues which concern us, but also in the spirit of justice, extend our hand to fellow Malaysians.

Secondly, Muslims must open up to a spirit of dialogue within the Muslim society as well as with the adherents of other faiths. Some confuse dialogue with agreement, but that is, of course, far from the truth! Dialogue exists because there are certain issues that we disagree on—such as matters of creed—but at the same time, we can find shared ground on the common challenges that we face. What is crucial is that ground rules for the dialogue must be set to provide an agreeable framework where the deliberation can take place in trust and confidence.

We have seen several dialogues in recent years which got into trouble for touching on what was deemed as 'sensitive' subjects. It goes without saying that it is crucial to involve genuine and authoritative scholars in these dialogues. If the objective is to find some point of understanding on the subjects, the different parties must be prepared to sit down and find rational ways to discuss them. Muslims must be prepared to listen to everyone as Islam has an impact on all Malaysians due to its status as the religion of the Federation.

Our Muslim authorities should be exposed to different ideas in order to cope with the changing world. In Singapore, the Islamic Religious Council invited former nun and controversial religious writer, Karen Armstrong, the Archbishop of Canterbury, Rowan Williams and a host of other contemporary intellectuals to talk to the Muslim authority. Initiatives like this build the confidence for Muslims to engage with different communities in a vibrant and diverse society. What does it say about the state of our Muslim community today if we cannot find individuals who are able to confidently and coherently engage with representatives from other communities?

However, great care must be taken to always bear in mind that the objective is not to stir unnecessary controversy, but to provide different perspectives and true understanding to all parties. Ultimately, this effort can often be sustained through working quietly, starting small and going back to the basics to avoid sensationalising the issue. This organic approach is a more sustainable one in seeking to build a conducive environment for Muslims to progress in a multi-racial community.

Thirdly, the institution of the *ulama'* must be kept independent from political interference. The difference between Islam and secularism is that Islam preaches that our religion and ethics must guide our public involvement. Politics is rife with compromises and moral hazards, and religion provides a useful spiritual compass. The institution of the *ulama'* must be kept independent to provide checks and balances on our politicians.

More often than not, ignorant authorities control the *ulama'* and politicise the institution to become mere rubberstamps to their policies. At the same time, we must be wary of reducing religion to just ideology as some literalists keep doing: they should be reminded how scholars of the past refused to be involved with political authority for fear that they would lose their precious intellectual and theological independence. This spurred a creative and lively culture that was the cornerstone of Islamic civilisation.

Sheikh Abdul Hakim Murad, a British convert who studied at Cambridge, Al Azhar and Oxford, said in an interview with the Australian Broadcasting Corporation in 2004:

> If you look at the Iranian experience, after 25 years of Islamic rule, their Ministry of Religious Guidance recently published figures that show that only 3 percent of Iranians now attend Friday prayers. Before the Revolution, it was almost 50 percent. So what kind of Islamic reformation

and revival has that actually delivered? Religion is now identified with a kind of prison, the pan-optician idea of the man at the centre of the State looking at everybody, Calvin's city of glass, nobody being able to misbehave in a way that annoys the clerics or the *mullah*s without calling down on them, not just the sanction of heaven, but the repressive capacities of the modern corporate State.

This does not mean that the *ulama* should not join politics, but they must be wary of going down the slippery slope of authoritarianism and the compromises that they make in the realm of politics.

Fourthly, we must continue to instil in the youth holistic religious values through accessible and creative ways—not just the legalistic rights and wrongs but also ethics, culture and spirituality. Too often, the young feel that religion is something stifling or removed from their daily concerns and therefore, choose to avoid it as much as they can. At the same time, those without exposure to the genuine teaching of Islam can be overzealous when they 'rediscover' Islam through misguided groups or erroneous sheikhs. Some believe banning these groups is the answer, but that is no longer effective in today's world. We must engage the younger generation, while genuine and competent scholars must provide a comprehensive, practical and flexible framework for the youth to serve as a guide for them in addressing daily concerns.

For example, mosques in Singapore are encouraged to have youth-designated areas as well as youth development officers to engage with the younger generation. There is also encouragement for younger *imam*s and *bilal*s (a positive development that is also happening in Malaysia) to allow them to connect with the youth. In Britain, in response to the influence of extreme groups among young British Muslims, scholars such as Tariq Ramadan, Sheikh Abdul Hakim Murad, Yemeni scholar Habib Ali al-Jifri, Bosnian Mufti Mustafa Ceric, former pop star Yusuf Islam (Cat Stevens) and Rwandan Mufti Saleh Habimana have worked together with FOSIS, Young Muslims Organisation and the British government for the Radical Middle Way initiative to inspire young people to become agents of change in their local communities.

We should also get more of our children to become religious scholars. For so long, many Malay parents prefer their brightest children to become doctors, lawyers, engineers and accountants but hesitate for them to become part of the *ulama'*. As a result, many of the brightest and most motivated youth are not included in religious training and education. This has changed steadily following the Islamic revival movement in the 1970s, but we need to ensure it becomes truly sustainable to give birth to a dynamic religious establishment.

NO COMPULSION:
NON-MUSLIMS AND ISLAM IN MALAYSIA

Article 3 of the Federal Constitution establishes Islam as the religion of the Federation, while other religions can be freely practised in peace and harmony. Article 11 provides for the freedom of all citizens to profess and practise his religion as well as propagate it, subject to certain limitations with regards to propagating to Muslims.

But religion can be a controversial issue in Malaysia, as it is elsewhere. The situation in Malaysia is further complicated by the fact that the racial dichotomy of Malay versus non-Malay is in line with the Muslim versus non-Muslim dichotomy. This is because Malays must be Muslim and form the dominant majority of the Bumiputera.

Hence, it is unsurprising that non-Muslims have genuine concerns with regards to their place in Malaysian society, especially since the 1970s when the Islamic revival took place. Muslims must appreciate that just as issues of conscience are sensitive to Muslims, it is just as important to non-Muslims as well.

As mentioned earlier, space for dialogue between Muslims and non-Muslims must be created, even for so-called 'sensitive' issues. If it has to be held behind the glare of the public to avoid unnecessary antagonism and misunderstanding, then by all means do it in that way. Muslims might not agree with what is being said by the non-Muslims, but we must have the compassion to listen to it, and the courage to provide our perspective convincingly. Muslims must not resort to hooliganism and violence to dispel these views.

With the Internet and globalisation, there are other ways to access these views anyway, and it can only be countered if we have the courage to defend our conviction. Recently, this took a further twist as many Malays who have little, if any, knowledge on Islam wanted to manipulate religion for political mileage by trying to 'out-Islamicise' each other. They cynically regard religion as a tool to further segmentise the Malaysian public.

What the Constitution espouses, however, is not a Western construct; rather it reflects a long-held principle within Islam that there is no compulsion in religion. Islam does not allow Muslims to force non-Muslims to become Muslims, the believers, however, are mandated to subscribe to a certain value system.

This is crucial. Those who seek to remove Muslims from that value system will find that they can never sufficiently do so; in fact, it only opens the door for the exact opposite to take place, for dangerous literalists to gain support and influence. It is Islam's established framework of scholarship and hierarchy of knowledge—founded on the Quran, the traditions of the Prophet, the consensus of the *ulama'* and adoption of non-conflicting customs—that has provided a source of moderation among Muslims.

Hence, it is important to defend not only the status of Islam as the religion of the Federation but also the Shariah Court system within the Malaysian judicial system that reflects the historical consensus that established our Federal Constitution. In order to provide the Shariah Court with necessary stature to reflect our Constitution, Article 121(1a) was rightly amended in 1988 to provide finality to Shariah Court decisions.

In recent years, this has come under challenge following disputes with regards to conversion both in life (such as the Azlina Jailani @ Lina Joy saga) and death (such as the Mohamed bin Abdullah @

Moorthy case). Again, so much controversy was created, but little was done to emphasise the main principle in question: the due process of our legal system as established by the Federal Constitution.

The conversion to Islam comes under the purview of Shariah Courts. Logically, any attempts to leave Islam must be made within the Shariah Courts in itself. Admittedly, there needs to be greater attention given to improve the mechanism to look into these matters to fulfil our jurisprudential principles in light of the complexity of a multicultural and modern society.

I believe that there is nothing wrong for the authorities to involve the various stakeholders to initiate such a discussion without compromising on Article 121(1a). There is, in my mind, no contradiction between maintaining the independence of the Shariah Courts and also ensuring that the non-Muslims of Malaysia are treated equitably. For example, in the case of a dispute of conversion such as the Moorthy case, how can we provide his spouse, who is a non-Muslim and thus not subject to the Shariah Court, the avenue to make her case?

These are the hard questions that we, as Muslims, should be asking ourselves rather than automatically dismissing such concerns. We must always seek to do justice to our fellow men and women, regardless of their religious faith.

At the end of the day, we must acknowledge that the law is only a last resort to solve our woes. An approach that is purely legalistic is out of sync with the tradition of mercy established since the time of the Prophet Muhammad. At times, we seem to be more obsessed about meting out punishment without taking into account its efficacy. Our concern, rather, should be with increasing the understanding between the people of all faiths.

THE SOCIAL REVOLUTION

MARRIAGE AND FAMILY LIFE

Traditionally Malay weddings were huge affairs, involving not only the extended family but everyone in the *kampung*. A huge wedding feast was normally prepared through *gotong-royong* where every member of the community contributed in his or her own way. When there were no modern amenities like television and life was tough, this was an event everyone looked forward to.

Girls married early, mostly in their teens. My mother married when she was 19 while my father was 29. My grandparents married even earlier (Tok Wan Jah, my maternal grandmother joked that she married at 18—which was considered late in the 1930s—because she was not attractive!). Like many women before and during her time, my mother did not further her studies after marriage and became a full-time housewife while my father worked as a civil servant.

Today, weddings are more commercialised. Urban Malays generally resort to hiring caterers to prepare the food. Many who live in cramped urban conditions rent halls to accommodate the guests, while more affluent Malays host their weddings in hotel ballrooms. Most Malays these days marry later and the trend is for both spouses to work. Even my mother's younger sisters completed their higher education and most of them had their own careers.

Yet, in spite of all the changes, marriage remains an integral institution in Malay society. Once you step into your thirties without being married, there is great social pressure to find you a prospective partner, especially if you are a woman. You get dragged along to family functions and the first thing your relatives will ask is inevitably, *"Bila nak kahwin?"* (When are you getting married?) Come to think of it, this is probably an ordeal that all single young adults in Malaysia have to undergo!

Thankfully, I anticipated this very early and decided to get married when I was 23! My wife, a year younger than me, was still studying when we got married and this was by no means a rarity amongst the Malays.

Marriage and the family institution, however, face new pressures and challenges. The loosening ties of the extended family, the influence of modern technology and global society, the pressures of the workplace on the marriage all add up to present a formidable set of challenges. Divorce is now on the rise as it becomes more socially acceptable, placing more children in broken families.

The role of family in providing a stable foundation for children to be nurtured comes under challenge. Parents do not have the same influence over their children, but expectations remain the same. When the influence of parents breaks down, we see social ills such as *mat rempit*, drug abuse, crime and pre-marital sex spread across our society.

As this becomes more serious, there is great expectation for the authorities to step in. Undoubtedly, they have a role to play. Everyone needs to play a role—government, the police, the local authorities, the mosque and the immediate community. But the central role of the family cannot be disputed.

Modernity's challenge to the family institution comes in the form of weakening its role in providing welfare, basic education, moral and ethical upbringing as well as much-needed love and support to the young. This can be seen in the development of the universal education system, the welfare state, pop culture and subsequently, a globalised market place. In many ways, these developments have contributed to an improvement—at the very least in the material sphere—of our life.

Liberalism, as a progressive force, made many contributions in advancing the position of women, ethnic and religious minorities and ultimately, the individual in the 20th century. At the same time, we have seen, not just in our community but across the world, that there is a point where modern society breaks down, and where modern institutions and mechanisms fail to provide a panacea. Previously, the favoured approach was the state; now it is the market—in order to provide a one-size-fits-all cure to social ills.

We need to step back and ask if there is a risk, in our zeal to embrace everything that is modern, that we might inadvertently destroy the old-fashioned values and institutions that have, and can continue to have, positive contributions to modern society. There needs to be a realisation that a strong family institution has an important role to play. This is not just some obscure 'Asian value' but something that is relevant to modern society globally.

Beyond the individual, the state (including our habit of relying on legislation) and the market, the family too, can play an important role in inculcating economic independence, a strong spiritual, ethical and moral fibre and a sense of concern for society. At the same time, I am not saying that family is a magic pill, an instant cure to all that is wrong in modern society.

There are, after all, broken and dysfunctional families, which can be more disastrous than a crumbling state or an inefficient market. All I am saying is that while we emphasise on the other institutions and mechanisms in society, we should not neglect the role of the family.

The family can have a positive contribution in the individual's interaction with society, the state as well as the global market. We've all heard the cliché, 'Mothers know best', but you know what? It's true. The fact is, in many instances, the whole family (not just mothers) knows what is best for a particular individual—better than an impersonal bureaucrat or a selfish businessman.

The family understands the context which the individual operates in, in most cases, much better than other institutions. The integral role played by the family in Malay society needs to be enhanced as we face the 21st century.

In this new scenario, the state cannot do everything, but it can do something and it should encourage a vibrant and independent family institution. While in certain countries there is a need to encourage family planning to keep population growth manageable, many developed countries have realised that they now need to encourage families to have children to sustain the economy.

There is still room for the state to play its role: Firstly, they can provide more opportunities for poorer families by providing allowances based on their income and number of children; secondly, they can nurture a flexible environment for working parents to bring up children; and thirdly encourage more facilities that are family-oriented. An efficient education and health sector can play an important supporting role to the family institution.

This is where I differ from the assertions of the neo-liberals. Even with globalisation, the government can continue to play the role in creating opportunities, even if not in the conventional one-size-fits-all statist approach. The key is to always ensure that the dignity of the individual and the dynamism of his or her society come first in everything done to or for them.

SUFFER THE YOUNG

Young Malays are always reminded that they are the generation that will inherit the mantle of leadership in the country; yet they are also frequently told that they are its biggest problems. The hypocrisy of this sort of double-speak is self-evident. The establishment unfortunately frames the discourse with little regard to the aspirations and concerns of the youth.

Who are the young Malays in the first place?

While there is a grave danger of generalising too much, there are certain commonalities between the young Malays and indeed all Malaysians of our generation, i.e., the Gen Y or 'Millennials'. These include, but are not limited to: our connectedness and utilisation of the Information Technology revolution; the opportunities that our parents or grandparents never had with the advent of the NEP and the modernisation of our economy; a political consciousness defined by Tun Dr Mahathir Mohammad's long reign and the dismissal of Datuk Seri Anwar Ibrahim.

On the downside, many consider our generation to be politically apathetic. Compared to the students of the 1960s and 1970s, it may certainly seem that our students appear far more compliant.

These very broad features have given birth to young Malays and Malaysians that are tech-savvy, more cynical and averse to authoritarian politics. Of course, there are many different class, ethnic and geographical variations to these themes, but the very diversity of the young Malaysia is in itself a commonality.

On the other hand, our generation is also facing severe challenges. These include our messy education system, low-wage economy, racial polarisation, cynicism towards the very concept of public service and the lack of credible young leaders.

The state of our education system means that opportunities for social mobility and employment are increasingly limited. Our universities are churning out more graduates, but our economy has stagnated in the value chain and is over-reliant on the low wages of foreign workers, meaning that there are less high-value jobs to go around. Living costs have increased dramatically, with only a marginal increase in wages, resulting in lower real wages.

Job satisfaction is at an all-time low as well. You know that canard about how young Malaysians are fussy about jobs? That's actually us reacting against exploitative work conditions that are growing more toxic daily, which stifle individual initiative and enterprise. Thus, more youths are burdened with study loans and a lack of jobs that meet their expectation as a result of university education. Our youths find it increasingly difficult to get a start in life in the way our parents did with the same qualifications.

As a result, many young Malays continue to consider government employment as the ideal job because of its security. I remember being part of a panel at the Selangor State Secretariat, Shah Alam interviewing applicants for an administrative assistant position that required a basic SPM or Diploma qualification. Many of the applicants who showed up, however, possessed degrees and one even had an MBA! The implication of this was that their abilities, as well as those of other graduates, have not been developed in other fields such as business, academia or NGOs, which in turn reinforces the culture of dependency on the state, a situation which is endemic in the community.

Conversely, there's the issue of the brain drain: many young

Malaysians, (with Malays joining the exodus in large numbers now) are choosing to migrate to get more fulfilling jobs and better quality of life overseas. We are the poorer without their talents and this is more often than not due to our socio-political stagnation.

Furthermore, the worsening racial polarisation in our public institutions has also affected young Malays. As a result, many Malays, including those brought up in urban settings, are worryingly unable to function in a plural society. These gaps are also becoming increasingly intra-racial and no longer merely inter-racial; surely a recipe for disaster in the years to come.

The troubles that our democracy went through since the 1980s coupled with the increasing authoritarianism have left many young Malaysians cynical, even disillusioned with the concept of public service. The lack of proper channels to voice their views brought about by laws such as the University and University Colleges Act (UUCA) has further emasculated what ought to be our natural outlets for political expression. No wonder apathy reigns.

More damaging, however, is the lack of credible young leaders and political consciousness amongst young Malaysians. For the former, the leadership of youth wings in political parties often becomes a means for power and profit, rather than a platform for genuine activism. For the latter, the same prevents the young people from becoming a voice and force in Malaysian politics.

With all these challenges in mind, it is easy to see why many are very downbeat on the prospects of our young people. But let us never doubt our potential to make a difference for our country. The 8 March 2008 Elections, where many young Malaysians voted for the first time in their lives, demonstrated what activist-minded and determined Malaysian youth can do. Mind you, that was just a small fraction! Where our predecessors took to the streets, we are now using Youtube, Facebook and blogs with equal if not more devastating effect.

The key, therefore, is to ensure that this momentum is not lost and that the socio-political awakening of young Malaysians continues unabated. Towards that end, progressive political forces in Malaysia need to embark on a Youth Empowerment Agenda to allow young Malaysians to join the forces for positive change in Malaysia. To my mind several areas need immediate attention.

First, we need to consider lowering the voting age to 18 and increasing genuine (and not BTN-inspired) civic/citizenship education in our schools. Secondly, we have to affect the repeal of the UUCA and other draconian laws or practices that stifle freedom of expression. Thirdly, political parties have to empower their youth wings and be more responsive to young voters. Keadilan's decision in 2009 to lower the youth wing's age limit to 35 years old is a case in point. While some youth leaders did not support the proposal, it was approved all the same and signalled how younger Malaysians will be given the space and room to contribute to the country.

Fourthly, our economic strategies must strengthen young families and the proper development of human capital. More money should be invested in better universities, while skills-based training should be expanded for their alternatives.

More importantly, young Malaysians need to stand up and be counted. The country desperately needs a clean break from the past and the youth must lead the way forward. Where there is division and racialism, we must stand united. Where there is cynicism, we must never falter in our idealism and incorruptibility.

But we also need to be involved. We have to register to vote, get our friends who have not done so to do so and actually head to the ballot boxes when the time comes. We need to close the gaps and break down the barriers that still exist between us.

This is the challenge that has to be put to the Malaysian youth and to their leaders. The latter too, must hold themselves to the highest standards in all areas for indeed they have the most exacting of constituencies!

It may seem like a thankless, futile job but there is the future of an entire country at stake. The youth of Malaysia need help, but sooner or later, they must also stand up for themselves. The young Malays too, must strive to inspire their compatriots of all races and be inspired in return. We are all not only called to action, but also to greatness. *The choice is ours.*

A GLIMPSE INTO SERI SETIA

I suppose I should mention a bit about my work as a State Assemblyman. The constituency I represent, Seri Setia, is located in the Kelana Jaya parliamentary constituency. Much of Seri Setia is under the Petaling Jaya City Council, but a small part of it falls under the purview of the Shah Alam City Council.

Demographics-wise, Malay voters constitute about 54.3 percent, Indians 28.3 percent and Chinese 16.3 percent. Sprawling bungalows are located in SS7 Kelana Jaya and Glenmarie, Shah Alam. Former Seafield and Glenmarie estate workers and Sunway miners live in terrace houses while former squatters from Kampung Lindungan, Kampung Penaga and Kampung Gandhi have been relocated to low-cost flats, including Desa Mentari.

It is truly a diverse constituency that represents the entire spectrum of Malaysian society. For years, the area was solidly BN, which efficiently gerrymandered it every 10 years to ensure that any shift in voting patterns would not affect BN's chances. In fact, in light of the backlash among Malay voters during *Reformasi*, the boundaries were shifted to ensure that it would be a mixed constituency, which was perceived as BN strongholds. In 2004, the BN candidate won with an 11,141 majority.

As I became active in Keadilan Kelana Jaya, I was introduced to the community living in the low-cost flats. The flats were built as part of the previous state government's 'Zero-Squatter' policy. As elaborated previously, they ignored many planning requirements in terms of density, provision of community halls and places of worship. When the residents demanded for *surau*s to be erected, playing fields were reduced to accommodate the *surau*s. This, in turn, angered the Indians who were not provided with adequate land for temples. The children of Desa Mentari, who are tired of cramped spaces, spend their time outdoors. The boys scramble for the limited futsal courts. As they flock around those of the same race, some of the juvenile fights they inevitably get into can spark off racial tensions as their parents and neighbours get involved.

As they grow older, they risk engaging in more illicit activities. A persistent problem among the Malay community is drug addiction that opens the door to other crimes and this sometimes happens in Seri Setia as well. These social ills and the difficult nature of life in urban Malaysia often take their toll on the residents here.

Cik Jah is one of them. She is from Kelantan and is married to an Indonesian contract worker. Her husband frequently falls ill and when he does, she resorts to feeding their children only two meals a day to keep costs low. Public transport is poor and they do not have money to pay for the school bus. Thus, the children walk along the highway each day, crossing a busy flyover to get to their school. I don't need to tell you how dangerous this is!

Cik Jah is by no means the exception. Many struggle each month to pay off their housing loans. Some resort to *ah long*s (loan sharks) with their outrageous interest rates to get by from month to month, and ultimately fall into a vicious cycle of debt. They come to my constituency office seeking to ask banks to postpone auctioning off their homes, and all I can do is to call the banks to give them some respite. This is a living example of the challenges of urban poverty that is now the biggest problem affecting not just the Malays but Malaysians in general. In the 1970s, the government allowed squatters to proliferate as it was felt this was a way for poor Malays to have access to urban amenities including better jobs and better schools. But the urban poor do not have access to land and livestock or to a cohesive community—the way that those in the *kampung*s do—that can provide relief in times of difficulty.

For decades, UMNO had cultivated the myth that they were the ones that UMNO was fighting for. But as the years passed by, they grew more and more disillusioned. When their squatters were replaced with low-cost flats, even the allocation of units was used as tools of patronage by the UMNO branch leaders. Those who chose not to support UMNO were sidelined.

On the other hand, the concerns of the Malays in the more affluent areas of Seri Setia differ slightly. There is a similar concern for rising crime, but they also have a higher expectation of the local authorities. They demand better public amenities, including recreational facilities.

Nurhaliza and Mazlan happen to be my friends from college who also live with their young son in my constituency. Both graduated from the University of London and now work in two GLCs. They came to my office one night to voice out the lack of quality pre-school facilities in the area. They also came to a crime dialogue I organised. Later, their house was broken into and the thief ran off with their valuables. They live in an older part of my constituency, dotted with single-storey terrace houses. Unlike newer developments, it is not a gated-community. They spoke of their frustration at the level of security in open-access neighbourhoods such as theirs.

The aspirations of the Malay community in Seri Setia—whether those of the working class or the affluent—generally correspond to those of their Malaysian counterparts in the neighbourhood and elsewhere in the country. It is interesting to note how similar we all are when you get down to the basics, even though we may be incredibly diverse.

It is an honour to represent the people of Seri Setia and I am humbled that they have chosen me to do so. While I do not know where the future may take me politically, the area has undoubtedly become my home. It will always hold a special place in my heart and I will continue to serve its residents as long as it is within my power to do so.

CONCLUSION

THE DREAM THAT IS MALAYSIA

Whenever I raise the points from this book in conversations, many Malays acknowledge its noble intentions, but at the same time, argue that it is too idealistic and not reflective of the reality.

It is fine to talk about equality, they say, but the other races are not fair to us anyway. They contend that equality is only relevant when it is useful for one's argument. They argue that equality is only useful when one is the victim—when it is to one's benefit not to be equal, one should discard equality as a consideration. So why bother?

It goes without saying that there are racists, bigots and chauvinists from all communities. Whenever non-Malays point out the discriminatory nature of the system in Malaysia, they should also acknowledge the discriminatory nature of small- and medium-sized industries in the country. They should also acknowledge that certain non-Malays benefit from the status quo through political connections and Ali-Baba partnerships.

Race will always be an important part of one's identity. Across the world, race remains a point of contention even in states where there are no ethnic-based privileges or affirmative action. For instance, in Singapore, which purportedly practises meritocracy, the government has different community funds for the different races, such as the Mosque Building and Mendaki Fund for the Malay-Muslim community.

In addition, while socio-economic factors play a major factor in shaping one's opportunities to succeed, culture does play a role—for example, there has been much analysis on Protestant and Confucian ethics vis-à-vis economic and political development. The link between culture and race is obviously more apparent than in other areas.

Different cultures influence different approaches to education and occupation, whether one's wealth is spent on immediate gratification or saving for a rainy day, whether entrepreneurship or job security is more valuable. But two important caveats must be made: first, it is important not to overstate the link; and second, having race-based affirmative action conditions different responses in different cultures as well.

It is also difficult to push the ethnic argument too far as the definition of Malay leaves blurred boundaries, more often than not determined by the bureaucrat's interpretation of the Constitution and national policy, coloured by their own preconceptions and prejudices. Furthermore, even in homogenous countries, other cleavages exist. Had Malaysia been entirely Bumiputera, then there might be problems between the recent immigrants from Indonesia and the local Malays, the Orang Asli and the tribes in Borneo. Or there might be differences between the Javanese and the Minangkabau. There might also be class differences.

If we were to visit Rwanda, which was embroiled in a genocide between the Hutus and Tutsis that left between 800,000 to 1,000,000 people dead, we would be hard pressed to distinguish between the two. The distinctions were accentuated by the Belgian colonialists between the locals who owned cattle and had long noses, and those who didn't. This sounds almost ludicrous, but it left a deadly legacy that divided the country.

I believe that as a country, we must move forward by protecting the rights of each and every Malaysian, moving the economy up the value chain and ensuring that the plight of the worst-off in society is addressed. Looking at the current system as a racial zero-sum game, in which Malays benefit and non-Malays suffer (or vice-versa) is pointless, as ultimately, it is the political elite who benefit at the expense of ordinary Malaysians of all races—a condition that is masked for the ordinary Malays beneath a veneer of racial superiority.

But the ethnic angle is still relevant for Malaysia to move forward. This is because it will only be possible if the dominant community—the Malays—can accept the need to do so. It is the Malays who hold political power and it is the Malays who are given the impression that they will lose more from a change in the system. Rather than designing a system that is based on the lowest common denominator of the worst of each community, we should design one that is fair to all and brings out the best in each of us.

Our challenge is to tell the ordinary Malays on the ground that we are on their side. We want to tell the Malay farmer struggling to earn a living that we are on his side. We want to tell the Malay factory worker living in an urban slum that we are on her side.

To Malays and Muslims, I say, bearing witness to the truth of Islam, we should not descend to extremism, but seek to uphold justice and be an example and a blessing to all human beings as advocated by our faith. Human beings are given a choice to do good and bad, and Muslims should know that we are always required to occupy the moral high ground.

Whither the Malay agenda, then? Let's not fool ourselves any longer. The Malay agenda, Malay unity and of course, the crowning glory, Malay supremacy, only assumes significance whenever UMNO does badly in the polls.

In reality, while some progress has been made, the vast majority of the poorest Malaysians are still Malays, the gap between rich Malays and poor Malays has grown bigger while the abandonment of Bahasa Malaysia as a medium of instruction has condemned more Malays to be left behind. In fact, it is sections of the Malay elite that fan the exclusivist racial sentiments among the poor Malays to consolidate their rent-seeking while the welfare of their poorer kith and kin (who become the pawns in the elite pursuit of further benefit) are relegated to the backburner.

If we talk about the Malay agenda as perpetuating elite Malays to consolidate their hold on power while other Malays remain poor then, yes, I do not believe that we should continue to uphold this so-called 'agenda'. But if we talk about the Malay Agenda as driving the Malays as a whole to succeed in the globalised world, then I would be wholeheartedly behind this.

I am in no way belittling what we have achieved so far. In many respects, the choice to adopt the NEP was right and this contributed greatly towards addressing the racial inequality that plagued the country when it became independent.

But to now make the NEP a sacred cow that cannot be questioned does not uplift the Malays. It was not divine revelation, but the considered policy of honourable men who wanted the best for the Malays and ultimately Malaysia. The policy was right then, but we need to move on and face the realities of today. We need to find the best solution for Malaysians in this day and age.

There are two possible responses in light of where the NEP has failed—either a different policy is needed or the present policy needs more time to succeed.

We need to be able to think critically in order to find the best way forward to get the Malays to succeed in the 21st century. In this book, I have argued that change is necessary and adopting a new system is in the Malay interest. To be stuck in the politics of the past and a system that artificially protects us from competition is not in the Malay interest.

The emergence of a Malay middle class and the fact that the Malays, as a majority, have always dominated politics and government since Independence set us apart from the situation in Apartheid South Africa or segregation-era America, in spite of the dominance of the non-Malays in the commercial and professional sectors.

Furthermore, the non-Malays now do not know any other country, having been born in Malaysia into families who have been here for many generations. They regard Malaysia as their home. Why, then, are they still regarded as 'outsiders' or 'foreigners'? We need to realign our policies to today's reality.

It is important to reflect on the thoughts and perspectives of the architects of the NEP. They saw the state of the Malay community and felt the need to act. Yet, they also knew that the NEP was a compromise for a specific period, not to be implemented in perpetuity. They were exposed to a liberal education and a multiracial environment.

My father personified the unique ideals of this generation when he sent all his children to Christian missionary schools, in spite of hailing from a family of Muslim scholars and being known for his strong Malay (or rather, Kelantanese) views. Three of my elder sisters went to Bukit Bintang Girls School, the fourth was educated in Assunta while I studied at La Salle PJ for my primary education. His reasoning was simple: he understood the strong *esprit de corps* fostered by missionary schools as well as their multiracial nature. He felt it was dangerous for his children to grow up without knowing other children from other races and religions.

Earlier, as a roommate to Ramon Navaratnam (now Tan Sri) in University Malaya, my father impressed him due to the fact that while he was a rare breed of Malays in university who faithfully observed his religious requirements, he took pains to do so without making his non-Muslim roommate uncomfortable, even if just for a little while.

Ironically, some of today's leaders take the policy for granted and are less exposed to Malaysia's plural society. The rhetoric that they use would have shocked and disgusted the architects of the NEP themselves, as I wrote earlier.

We can continue relying on preferential quotas and subsidies at the expense of other Malaysians. But while it might please us to continue receiving these privileges, they do not actually benefit us if they continue to hold us back from competing with the rest of the world or producing the best Malays to move us forward. Our existing policies have held us back from keeping pace with Singapore, Taiwan and Korea—all countries that in 1960 were earning similar levels of per-capita income as us. Now the per-capita incomes of these countries are 500, 300 and 200 percent respectively, more than Malaysia's.

It is baffling that the Malays are so intent on arguing that the NEP has failed in order to perpetuate the policy as evident in the Lim Teck Ghee controversy. Was it not a tragedy when UMNO leaders competed with one another to say how the NEP, UMNO's pet policy, has been a failure?

The NEP was about far more than just equity. It was about the creation of a Malay middle class and the eradication of poverty. It is because the NEP has been generally successful in allowing the Malays to make huge strides that we now need a different approach in facing the new challenges of an increasingly globalised environment. On the other hand, the perpetuation of the NEP in a deteriorating democratic space and the demise of checks and balances allowed corruption to fester as economic and political power became dangerously fused by the political elite.

A race-centric system is fundamental for the survival of any race-based political parties. This explains why UMNO leaders have continued propagating the relevance and desirability of a race-centric system: without such a system, UMNO's political hegemony would collapse. A policy of race-based affirmative action that only benefits the politically-dominant majority exposes us to a slippery slope, where the policy becomes entrenched for the benefit of the political elite, instead of for the truly-deserving.

Even from a purely utilitarian perspective, promoting a system that decouples affirmative action from race and instead focuses on socio-economic status will continue to primarily benefit Malays, as we form the growing bulk of the country's population, as well as a majority of the marginalised. The Constitutional position of Islam, the Malay Rulers and the Malays will continue to be preserved as there are safeguards against amending the relevant Constitutional provisions while Malays are a growing majority in the country. In no way am I advocating a winner-take-all scenario where those who cannot compete are left behind.

Acknowledging that many challenges remain in creating Malay entrepreneurs to succeed in a globalising world, I have argued that Malays should rely less on government intervention while more should instead be done by successful Malay entrepreneurs to set aside some of their wealth to help other members of the community to move forward. This, coupled with a government emphasis on building genuine Malay and non-Malay business ventures, will go a long way towards building a sustainable framework for Malay entrepreneurs to move up the value chain and become competitive in the globalised environment.

If the Malays in London, Dubai and New York, who are small minorities who do not enjoy preferential policies or dominance in politics, can succeed and progress, what is stopping the Malays in Malaysia from moving towards a more open environment that is less obsessed with race as a divider? The country needs a new narrative.

While this book is focused on addressing what the Malay community as well as the government need to do in order for the community to move forward, other Malaysians too need to play a role for change to succeed. By assisting more Malays to participate in business as genuine entrepreneurs, pushing for positive change in the vernacular school system and accepting the need to master Bahasa Malaysia as the national language, the non-Malays can win a lot more goodwill among the Malay community to support changes to the status quo.

At the end of the day, to move forward will require all communities—Malay and non-Malay—to play their part in focusing on developing the country in a fair and holistic manner for all, so that Malaysia can reach its potential to develop and at the same time remain true to its colourful heritage. Malaysia would be a better place when the different races are willing to stand up for one another.

It is crucial that the shift is done gradually to ensure that Malays do not experience a sudden sense of losing out from change. When the Soviet Union collapsed the Washington consensus advocated 'shock therapy' for the transition of the command economy into a market economy. But this resulted in an economic crisis and untold misery for its people, ultimately sacrificing many of the gains made as a result of reform, including the democratic institution itself. Therefore, we must accept that the change in the system must be managed at a moderate pace. Hence, in the proposals I have outlined in this book, I seek to balance idealism with pragmatism. Clearly, however, the status quo is not an option.

In fact, it is the rising inequality and sense of marginalisation as a result of globalisation and liberalisation that rendered Francis Fukuyama's *The End of History and the Last Man*—which argued that economic liberalisation and political democratisation would be the ultimate global settlement—a pipe dream. Just as the same combination in Malaysia's early years led to the 13 May 1969 riots, this has fuelled the violent breakdown of other nation states. Social cohesion is an important precursor to democracy.

Some quarters might dismiss my views as being typical of a middle-class Malay youth, who has reaped the benefits of the NEP and is now biting the hand that fed him. I cannot deny that I am a beneficiary of the NEP. Yet, it is a testimony of how far the NEP has succeeded that its beneficiaries are now arguing for change. The birth of a Malay middle class has made change inevitable.

Just as the Malay leaders had the courage to implement the NEP to uplift the Malays in the '70s—a policy that was right for its time, we now need the courage to find the best way to deal with today's challenges and complexities. The Malays in the 21st century must have the confidence to grapple with differing views and opinions from within the country and without.

Stifling these views or running amok must no longer be our response. Choosing to let our emotions dominate and have a prevailing siege mentality will not help. Malaysians, including Malays today, are more questioning and critical. We must learn to deal with the situation rationally and intellectually. We need to think long and hard about the best way to move forward.

It is interesting to note that Datuk Seri Najib Tun Razak, the son of the creator of NEP, introduced a slew of policy reforms after assuming the leadership of the country in 2009. He accepted the premise of our call for change—which a few years ago was branded as a betrayal to the Malays. Although he liberalised aspects of the policy, he did not deal with governance and social justice. In order to move forward, these changes need to be viewed beyond politics; they must be viewed as reforms that we must embrace for the betterment of our society.

Even in moving forward, difficult challenges will remain for our diverse society. The rapidly changing world means that different challenges will emerge in swift succession. Changing our approach will better equip us to deal with these changes. At the very least, we will be looking ahead, instead of being mired in the past.

We can seek a new consensus for our society in the coming years so that the nation will not be left behind. The Malays and all Malaysians for that matter can only survive if we develop organically and are less reliant on top-down frameworks. We can then at least leave our children with a society imbued with a sense of decency, dignity and fair play that goes a long way towards fulfilling the dreams of our founding fathers.

POSTSCRIPT

TO MOVE MALAYSIA FORWARD

How well has *Moving Forward* "aged" considering all that has happened?

When I ponder this question, I am reminded of what the late Chinese premier Zhou Enlai allegedly said in the early '70s when he was asked about the impact of the French Revolution: "It is too soon to say."

I do want to stress that what I have advocated in this book is not necessarily the best or only way to resolve the challenges facing the Malay community. But I do believe that these challenges need to be addressed, and in a progressive manner at that.

The Malays must embrace progress

The message of *Moving Forward* is this: The Malay community needs to embrace democracy, progressive politics and diversity. This is the right thing to do as well as the only way to ensure the survival of our race, religion and country.

It is also something that all Malaysians must back because the country can only be a freer, more equitable and prosperous place if the Malay community feels secure. Like it or not, the reforms that we need for such outcomes will not succeed unless the Malays are onboard.

Authoritarianism, even in the name of necessary reform (if such a thing is even possible), will fail in Malaysia, all the time, every time. This is because Malaysians—for all our seeming deference to power—fundamentally cherish liberty.

This is true for all the races and especially the Malays. For better or for worse, people do not like to be told what to do.

What (actually) went wrong?

Sadly, in 2019, it is apparent that the anxieties that a great many in the Malay-Muslim community felt in 2009 have remained, if not exacerbated.

Why has this happened? It is true that the Pakatan Harapan government could have acted in a more prudent, gradual fashion, especially for controversial issues like the ICERD (International Convention on the Elimination of All Forms of Racial Discrimination). And the task of national unity and integration is one that must be borne equally, by all Malaysians.

But there is little chance that the non-Malays—even if they wanted to—can succeed in displacing the Malays (and let's be frank, almost all of them don't want to). And as demographic shifts do their work, this will become altogether impossible.

At some point, we are going to have to stop blaming the other races and take a good, hard look at ourselves, or rather, at the decisions we have trusted Malay leaders to make on our behalf.

Why are there Bumiputeras who are still struggling despite decades of the NEP? Why is it that the social mobility that the NEP has brought seem so fragile at times and needs constant replenishment from the diminishing state coffers?

Why have intra-ethnic socio-economic disparities grown, especially in the Bumiputera community? Why is it more often than not it is the elites—Bumiputeras and non-Bumiputeras alike—that have benefitted most from various schemes to benefit the community?

Why do we Muslims seem more fearful and embattled even as the size of ummah continues to grow both in Malaysia and globally? Why have we become even more divided over theological points that were non-issues in the past? Why do some Malay-Muslims use religion to incite or exclude others?

Why have social ills like drug addiction and child abuse seemingly become more rampant in our community? Why are some Malays more interested in policing the bodies of women than in protecting the most vulnerable members of our community? Why have we not been able to challenge the most negative stereotypes against our community?

In short: Why do we feel stuck?

Lack of leadership is the problem

I believe the answer lies in leadership, or rather, the lack of it. If the Malays are less happy, secure, wealthy or educated now than they ought to be, then the fault lies with our leaders. Nothing—absolutely nothing—has been denied to the Malay elite.

If the community has not achieved much, it is because our leaders were corrupt or short-sighted. The ones who were neither moved too quickly or too slowly or unwisely.

Blame for the travails of the Malays rest, not with the non-Malays, or Pakatan Harapan, but with the actions of previous administrations, which employed racial as well as religious scaremongering and incitement in a bid to remain in power while neglecting their duty to truly uplift the community.

But the problem has not only been with our political, business and religious leaders. Ordinary Malays seem to have also become less accepting and open with each other, especially those of different socio-economic status.

The educated and wealthy embrace global ideas but risk losing touch with their roots. The less well-off remain vulnerable to populist demagogues or are unreasonably hostile to even positive, much-needed change.

Malays who speak or stand-out—especially the young—are vilified for trivial reasons. The Malays are often their own worst critics.

Urban and rural, rich and poor, locally and foreign-educated, religious and secular—the Malays are starting to drift apart. Often, there is impatience, suspicion and outright contempt for the other.

How can we expect to gain the respect of other Malaysians when we seem to hate each other so? I am not ignoring the discrimination and prejudice faced by the Malays as mentioned in the original edition of the book. Neither am I calling for our differences to be swept under the rug. There is now a wide spectrum of attitudes and approaches towards politics, religion and other issues in our community. Some leaders believe this is disastrous.

I don't.

The Malays must embrace diversity and democracy

It is not wrong to have different views, including on things like religion, language and culture. It would probably not serve our community well if we were monolithic on everything.

The real disaster is not being able to manage these differences. The real danger is in believing that our differences need to be conquered or eliminated, rather than negotiated, so that the race and hence, Malaysia, can progress.

This is why I believe the Malays need to embrace democracy and progressive politics. The community is simply too diverse now to be represented by just one party or ideology. Anybody who says that is basically asking the Malays to give them absolute power—which corrupts absolutely.

We have got to learn to live in a world where Malays may feel differently about certain issues and who may not all vote the same way. Perhaps we would be happier if we spent less time worrying about these things and focus on issues that matter, like making our country more prosperous and safer for everyone.

No one can seriously regard the 9 May 2018 General Elections as a loss of power for the Malays. Indeed, the Pakatan Harapan government has proven time and time again to be cognisant of the community's sensitivities. Power concentrated in the hands of one group of Malays doesn't necessarily mean the entire community is empowered. Rather, it simply facilitates that group's capacity for aggrandisement and corruption.

The new Malaysia should be an opportunity for the Malays to change themselves for the better via economic and political reform. It is not a time for fear or recrimination but for courage and self-renewal. Greater openness and transparency will in fact protect the community from many of the abuses that hurt it in the past. Witness the abuse and subversion of many Bumiputera-based institutions such as Tabung Haji and FELDA—these things happened because Malaysia did not have greater democracy and freedom.

Thankfully, the fact that a great many Malays chose to vote against the old government shows that our self-preservation instinct remains intact. The post-2018 order is a time for exciting possibilities for the Malays that must not be squandered. Democracy is a good thing for our people.

The world is changing and with it, new challenges

The Malays need not fear democratisation and they need not fear globalisation either. And to be honest, it really doesn't matter what we think about these things because the world is going to keep changing whether we like it or not.

It is unclear whether the so-called revival of authoritarian populism, which in part was a backlash against globalisation, will last or not.

But whatever happens, competition between the countries in the world for resources, trade and investment as well as geopolitical power will only continue, rather than abate. The Fourth Industrial Revolution will render many jobs obsolete.

The internet and social media have created new opportunities to communicate but also presents constantly-evolving security issues. And climate change threatens our very existence here on earth.

The Malays will not be able to survive, much less compete in this environment if they keep sliding back to the old UMNO-style of governance. The racialised, patronage-based state and zero-sum game mentality that it created will not be able to protect the Malays and Bumiputera indefinitely.

Indeed, it could be argued that such a style of governance held and continues to hold the Malays back. The 1Malaysia Development Berhad and other scandals were certainly not aberrations, but the natural conclusion of the old Malaysia's failure to embrace greater openness and democratic norms.

The result was the wholesale robbing of our country and its humiliation. And it has arguably challenged the very notion that the Malays should lead the country.

The so-called "crutches" of the past have brought us to a crossroads. The choice is between a limbo of mediocrity with eventual decline looming or to forge ahead—educationally, economically, politically and socially.

I know what I prefer, at least for me and my family.

What do we need to move forward?

But I don't want this to be just yet another book "scolding" the Malays and telling them how inadequate they are.

I never understood why some leaders tell the Malays that they are and must be supreme in the country, yet all the while carping on their supposed shortcomings.

That's not how you raise children to become self-confident and capable adults. And it won't work with an entire ethnic group either.

As the great Muslim sociologist and historian, Ibnu Khaldun wrote in the Muqaddimah: "Throughout history many nations have suffered a physical defeat, but that has never marked the end of a nation. But when a nation has become the victim of a psychological defeat, then that marks the end of a nation."

Let us not endure psychological defeat.

There's an old saying from the world of computers: garbage in, garbage out. I am not saying that we should have an inflated view of ourselves; that is certainly not warranted.

But we have also come a long way and there are many things that we can be proud of. Like our fellow Malaysians, you will find Malays all over the world succeeding in different fields and professions. Many have done so with little or no government help.

More importantly, we have our faith and our families. We cannot and should not measure the "success" of our ethnic group or country in purely materialistic terms. We should also measure it in terms of our happiness.

I am reminded of what Robert F. Kennedy once said in a speech:

> "Our gross national product ... does not allow for the health of our children, the quality of their education, or

the joy of their play. It does not include the beauty of our poetry or the strength of our marriages; the intelligence of our public debate or the integrity of our public officials. It measures neither our wit nor our courage; neither our wisdom nor our learning; neither our compassion nor our devotion to our country; it measures everything, in short, except that which makes life worthwhile."

Likewise, the success and happiness of the Malays does not necessarily rest solely on how much of the economy we control, how many doctors we produce or how many skyscrapers we own.

These are important things that all good Malaysian governments should pay attention to and be accountable for. But it will not—and cannot—be the things that bind us together, to make us confident, compassionate and dynamic people. As RFK noted, we cannot measure the inner life and health of a people solely through economics.

That is something I am not hearing much of. Which leader in Malaysia today truly cares about how happy the Malays, indeed, all Malaysians, really are? This is something that Pakatan Harapan must also pay attention to.

There's no point going on and on about the community's ills and what is holding us back. We're all aware of it: as I said, the Malays are often the first to admit their faults. Books and articles about the Malays and their problems have been written since colonial times.

It has and always will be a question about willpower. There is nothing in Malay culture and Islam that militates against us being outward-looking or progressive. Moreover, the idea that genetics or other biological factors can somehow impact an ethnic group's chances at success has long been discredited by science.

The problem is that we often pull ourselves back from correcting the problems that face us. The ICERD saga is just one example of such self-defeating behaviour.

We can debate and draft all sorts of policy solutions, but without the will to change, reform and survive, it will all be useless.

The question is: What do we need to do to go beyond this? To get the will to embark on change and stick to it?

To move the Malays—and Malaysia—forward?

The solution is also leadership

It goes back to leadership.

We need leaders who understand the complexities that the Malays and Malaysia face. Who can somehow balance the country's identity politics and the seemingly irreconcilable differences between its people.

There has lately sprung up this idea that good leadership in Malaysia must be brusque, take-no-prisoners and my-way-or-the-highway. This style of leadership may seem attractive or meme-worthy, but as I have argued, it is fundamentally out of step with Malaysia's true nature.

Leaders who try to mould their countries in their own image almost always fail. The country is always bigger than one man's vision for it.

Rather, the kind of leadership that Malaysia needs is one that combines the hopes and dreams of all its people, that overcomes all its fears. It is one that rejects both fanaticism and win-at-all-costs but embraces diversity.

It is always easier to insist that religion, ethnicity and culture be excluded from public life. But again, it goes against human nature. The key is to ensure that no one is sidelined because of it and that national unity is a journey we take together, rather than a race to the bottom of the lowest common denominators.

We need leaders who understand how to sequence reform, who know which battles to fight rather than thrive in conflict. And while socio-political reform must be gradual, reform must come sooner or later.

There must be a greater focus on making the economy work for all Malaysians. The focus must be on jobs, jobs, jobs. And the Malays must be prepared to face the globalised challenges I highlighted earlier.

Education must be made relevant to the needs of industry, free of political interference and accessible to all. The current Pakatan Harapan government's renewed interest in Technical and Vocational Education and Training (TVET) is certainly a welcome development.

And we must continue to not only protect our women from discrimination and harassment—but also harness their potential in the workforce and marketplace. Pakatan Harapan must continue to invest in the people—Bumiputera and non-Bumiputera.

Certainly, our spending needs to be more prudent and wastage eliminated. But when it comes to healthcare, education, public safety and transportation, the money can and must be found.

Austerity is death.

The Malays must lift each other up

But the Malays cannot simply be passive recipients of government handouts and opportunities. Rather, we must excel and expect the highest standards from ourselves.

There must be zero-tolerance for corruption, jobbery and venality. The community must jumpstart itself and police itself.

Let us continue to be our own fiercest critics. But that is not the same as being our own worst enemies. We must also lift each other up and urge each other on.

Malays who succeed and excel must help others to succeed and excel, especially the young and those from disadvantaged areas. Mentoring is something that all Malay entrepreneurs and professionals who have "made it" should do.

It should be second nature to them. The old African-American saying is apt in this circumstance: Each one, teach one.

The non-Malays are not our enemies either, but our fellow citizens. Their presence in Malaysia, as well as their practicing their faiths, languages and cultures, are not a challenge to our special position.

Instead, they are a reminder that along with rights, the Malays also have responsibilities: to unite the country and make it secure for everyone. There must be greater openness and trust all round.

We need leaders, not only in Parliament and the State Assemblies, but also our neighbourhoods, offices, educational institutions and places of worship, who can build rather than destroy this trust.

The choices ahead

This is the sort of leadership that Malaysia needs right now. And this is the sort of leadership that the Malays must provide.

A time may come when a non-Malay who can shoulder the weighty task will be called to do so. Until then, the Malays must step into the breach.

In many ways, what I have written now is not very different from what I wrote in 2009. I suppose this is something to be regretted as it perhaps highlights that little has changed despite all that the country has gone through in these last ten years. Whether or not we will be facing the same problems in 2029 and whether Malaysia will be a worse or better place then—or for the rest of the 21st century—depends on us and on the kind of leaders we choose.

It might be difficult, even impossible for the Malays to be able to constantly provide virtuous and capable men and women who can move Malaysia forward.

But we must try. And I know in my heart of hearts that we have it in us.

SELECT BIBLIOGRAPHY

Al-Akiti, Muhammad. (2005) *Defending the Transgressed by Censuring the Reckless Against the Killing of Civilians*. Birmingham: Aqsa Press & Hellenthal: Warda Publications.

al-Attas, Syed Hussein. (1977) *The Myth of the Lazy Native: A Study on the Image of the Malays, Filipinos and Javanese from the 20th Century and Its Function in the Ideology of Colonial Capitalism*. London: Frank Cass.

al-Attas, Syed Muhammad Naquib. (1978) *Islam and Secularism*. Kuala Lumpur: ABIM.

Ali, Syed Husin. (2008) *The Malays: Their Problems and Future*. Kuala Lumpur: The Other Press.

Allen, Graham, and Iain Duncan-Smith. (2008) *Early Intervention: Good Parents, Great Kids, Better Citizens*. London: The Centre for Social Justice & The Smith Institute.

Boestamam, Ahmad. (1972) *Dr. Burhanuddin: Putera Setia Melayu Raya*. Kuala Lumpur: Pustaka Kejora.

Faaland, Just; Jack Parkinson, and Rais Saniman. (2003) *Growth and Ethnic Inequality: Malaysia's New Economic Policy.* Kuala Lumpur: Utusan.

Gomez, Edmund Terence and Jomo K. S. (1999) *Malaysia's Political Economy: Politics, Patronage & Profits.* Cambridge: Cambridge University Press.

Ho Seng Ong. (1952) *Education for Unity in Malaya.* Penang: Malayan Teachers Union.

Ibrahim, Anwar. (1996) *Asian Renaissance.* Singapore: Times Editions.

Jaafar, Kamarudin. (2000) *Dr. Burhanuddin Al Helmy: Pemikiran & Perjuangan.* Kuala Lumpur: IKDAS.

Johan, Khasnor. (1996) *Educating the Malay Elite: The Malay College 1905-1941.* Kuala Lumpur: Pustaka Antara.

Leete, Richard. (2007) *Malaysia: From Kampung to Twin Towers.* Shah Alam: Oxford Fajar.

Lim Teck Ghee. (2006) 'Corporate Equity Distribution: Past Trends and Future Policy'. Accessed 13 December 2008 from <http://www.cpps.org.my/downloads/D_%20Corporate_Equity_Distribution.pdf>.

Mohamad, Mahathir. (1970) *The Malay Dilemma.* Petaling Jaya: Federal Publications.

Ong Kian Ming. (2008) 'Making Sense of the Political Tsunami', *Malaysiakini* (11 Mac 2008). Accessed 13 December 2008 from <www.malaysiakini.com/news/79604>.

Puthucheary, James J. (2004) *Ownership and Control in the Malayan Economy.* Kuala Lumpur: Insan.

Rahim, Lily Zubaidah. (1998) *The Singapore Dilemma: The Political and Educational Marginality of the Malay Community.* Shah Alam: Oxford University Press.

Ramadan, Tariq. (2003) *Western Muslims and the Future of Islam* Oxford: Oxford University Press.

Sen, Amartya. (1999) *Development as Freedom.* New York: Alfred Knopf.

Yusuf, Hamza. (2004) *Purification of the Heart: Signs, Symptoms and Cures of the Spiritual Diseases of the Heart.* Chicago: Starlatch Press.

Yusuf, Hamza, and Zaid Shakir. (2007) *Agenda to Change Our Condition.* Hayward: Zaytuna Institute.

ABOUT THE AUTHOR

Nik Nazmi Nik Ahmad is presently the Member of Parliament for Setiawangsa, elected Member of the KEADILAN Central Leadership Council and Chief Organising Secretary of the party.

He was born in 1982 in Kuala Lumpur and grew up in Petaling Jaya. He attended La Salle Petaling Jaya before attending MCKK and Kolej Yayasan UEM. He read law at King's College London on a PNB Scholarship.

He came back to Malaysia and worked at PNB before becoming private secretary to Anwar Ibrahim from 2006 to 2008.

Nik Nazmi was the youngest elected representative in the 2008 general election when he won the Seri Setia state seat in Selangor. He was political secretary to Selangor Menteri Besar Abdul Khalid Ibrahim until 2010 when he was appointed as KEADILAN's Communication Director. From 2013 to 2014 he was the Deputy Speaker of the Selangor State Assembly. He was elected as KEADILAN Youth Leader in 2014 and the first Pakatan Harapan Youth Leader in 2017.

In 2014 he was appointed as the Selangor State Executive Councillor for Education, Human Capital Development, Science, Technology and Innovation.